# CHILDREN ARE LISTENING

*What We Say Matters*

by

## SHAUNA F. KING
PARENT & EDUCATOR

© Copyright 2022 Shauna F. King

**All rights reserved.**

No part of this publication may be reproduced, distributed, stored, or transmitted in any form or by any means, including photocopying, recording, or other electronic or mechanical means, methods, or apps, without the prior written permission of both the copyright holder and the publisher of this book, except in the case of brief quotations embodied in critical reviews and certain other noncommercial uses permitted by copyright law. Please do not participate in or encourage electronic piracy of copyrighted materials. For permission requests, write to the author at shauna@shaunafking.com.

ISBN: 978-1-7362644-1-6

# ACKNOWLEDGEMENTS

*To my husband Mark and my children Matthew and Morgan, thank you for allowing me the space to write and for cooking dinner on the nights that I forgot.*

*To my parents, family, and church families whose prayers, words of encouragement, wisdom, and correction have guided me throughout my life. Although it may not have seemed like it then, yes, I was listening.*

*To my sister Sharonda, my colleagues and friends, Bryan, John, and LeAnn, thank you for listening to me as I talked about and stressed over this book. Your encouragement helped me finish it.*

*To DeAnna, thank you for always reminding me of Philippians 4:13. You will never be forgotten.*

*Children Are Listening*

# TABLE OF CONTENTS

Acknowledgements ................................................................. iii

CHAPTER ONE: The Power of Words ............................... 1

CHAPTER TWO: Relationship-Building Words .................. 9

CHAPTER THREE: OMG!!
(Optimism, Mindfulness, and Gratitude) ............................ 21

CHAPTER FOUR: Label Products, Not Children ............... 39

CHAPTER FIVE: What We Speak Starts in Our Mind ....... 47

CHAPTER SIX: Words Can Hurt ......................................... 59

CHAPTER SEVEN: Confidence Building Words ............... 71

CHAPTER EIGHT: Good Job and Other Words of Praise .. 85

CHAPTER NINE: Let's Talk about Behavior ..................... 91

CHAPTER TEN: Intent vs. Impact of Words ..................... 117

CHAPTER ELEVEN: Speaking Hope to Our Children ..... 125

Closing Words .................................................................. 135

37 Phrases Children Need to Hear from Adults ................. 139

References ...................................................................... 143

**CHAPTER ONE**

# THE POWER OF WORDS

*"If your friends told you to jump off a bridge, would you do it?"*
*"Money doesn't grow on trees."*
*"Don't you embarrass me!"*

Do you remember words or phrases your parents or family members said to you as a child? Maybe you remember some positive words like, "I love you," "You can do anything you put your mind to," or "I'm proud of you." Maybe you remember life lessons like, "Always finish everything on your plate because there are starving children in the world," "Money doesn't grow on trees," or "Treat others as you would like to be treated."

The words that we say to children become their inner voice. This inner voice stays with us throughout our lifetime, and it's a voice that children depend on consciously and subconsciously. It's the voice that, to this day, makes me cover my head when it is cold outside, tells me only to lend money I can afford not to get back, and reminds me to respect my elders. Sometimes, we even have stimulating words or phrases that we remember from the adults closest to us. Some phrases educators and parents remember and have shared in my workshops include, "Don't you make me pull this car over..." "Life isn't fair," or "Stop crying before I give you something to cry about!"

We remember these words and phrases because we were listening. There is also a good chance that we have repeated these phrases to our own children or students. Despite the common thought that children tune out everything that adults say, they are aware of the language and words that we use regularly with them. Our little children have big ears, and our adolescents take in more than they admit. Even when we think they can't or aren't paying attention, children hear us. This is something that adults should be aware of and take maximize the benefits of. I have two early memories of realizing my children were listening and paying attention to my words.

Story #1 - My children were seven and nine at the time, and we were on our way to soccer practice when we passed the Baskin-Robbins ice cream shop. My daughter, Morgan, asked in her sweetest high-pitched voice, "Mommy, can Matthew and I have ice cream after practice, please?" It's amazing how children remember how to be polite when they want a treat. I responded, "I'll think about it." Almost immediately, I overheard Morgan whisper to her brother, "Matthew, we're going to get some ice cream because 'I'll think about it' is adult language for Yes."

Story #2- I told my preschool age son Matthew that we had an appointment to see his doctor. "What's an appointment mommy?" he asked. I explained that an appointment was a special time set aside by the doctor to see him and only him. After arriving at the doctor's office, sitting in the waiting room for almost 45 minutes and watching our appointment time come and go, Matthew looked up at me and asked, "Mommy, does the doctor understand what the word appointment means?"

We each have a unique relationship with words. We hear them differently based on our experiences. What comes to mind when I say red? Some of us think of the red heart. A fire engine may come to mind for a child, a red state for a politician, and a negative balance on a company's financial statement for an accountant. Words can evoke deep-seated emotions or arouse childhood memories. When I was a young child, I thought the word corpse meant a model, as in a fashion model. It sounds crazy to think of a relationship between a corpse and a model, but it goes back to my early years of choosing my clothes for school. To persuade me to dress warmly for cold temperatures, my mother would make amusing remarks about the consequences of being underdressed for the weather. When I tried to wear a short-sleeved t-shirt or refused to wear a coat when it was cold, my mother would comment:

> "Shauna, you will be the best-looking corpse anyone has ever seen."

While these words may not sound flowery or even seem a bit dark coming from a mother to their child, it was neither a threat nor a reason to contact Child Protective Services. You must know my mom to understand the spirit of her words fully. My mother is the nicest, most thoughtful, caring person you will ever meet. She would give you her last dollar, come to your house to help you in a challenging situation, and write you a heartfelt thank-you note for any small gift you sent her. She is absolutely as kind as they come. This colorful phrase was probably passed down from previous generations. My grandmother probably uttered these words to my mother at some point during her childhood. Eventually, I got older, learned the definition of a corpse, and fully understood the meaning of her words. I didn't fear an untimely death because of my clothing choice, but when I hear the word corpse, I strangely revisit my early predictions of a possible future on a New York City Fashion runway.

Our language significantly impacts how children feel about themselves, how they relate to others, and how resilient they are in meeting challenges. Most parents and educators are exceptional in this area. There are exceptions, of course, and even the best and most affirming adults admit that they benefit from the reminder of their impact on children.

Dr. Maya Angelou was one of my all-time favorite authors and speakers. Dr. Angelou could do with words what very few others can. She was acutely aware of the power of words, which was one of the reasons she was so skilled at using them. In an interview with USA Weekend magazine, Dr. Angelou said, "I am convinced that words are things, and we simply don't have the machinery to measure what they are. I believe that words are tangible things... that words once said, do not die." In the same interview, Dr. Angelou made one of the most compelling statements about the impact of our words on others: "Words go into the body. So, they cause us to be well and hopeful and happy and high energy and wondrous, funny, and cheerful. Or they can cause us to be depressed. They get into the body and cause us to be sullen and sour and depressed and finally, sick." The fact that our words enter the body and immediately impact emotions, whether positive or negative, demonstrates that they have power.

Parents and educators work together to teach and guide our youth. Our messages to children are not always the same, but they are remarkably similar in many important ways. As an educator and a parent, I can appreciate how adults talk to children differently depending on whether we're at home or school, relating as family members or as members of a classroom community. Adult language can boost children's self-esteem, encourage them to care for others and provide them with the motivation to face challenges. I am hopeful that more adults will become acutely aware of the power of words since words can either uplift or tear down. What we hear as children shapes our character.

Throughout the book, I've included opportunities to focus on key takeaways and reflect on the information presented. I encourage you to take a moment to reflect and connect your thoughts with mine. You are free to agree or disagree, but I hope the conversation will spark positive thoughts and actions, leading to intentionality in our interactions with children. Language matters. It's just that simple.

## Takeaways

- Decades after our childhood ends, we remember the words adults used when speaking to us.
- Our language significantly impacts how children feel about themselves, how they relate to others, and how resilient they are in meeting challenges.
- Our use of language and words are important choices, and we make them every day.

## Pause for Reflection

What words or phrases do you remember that your parents or family said to you as a child?

_____
_____
_____
_____
_____
_____

Reflect on the quote from Dr. Maya Angelou. What types of words do you want coming into your own body and going into the bodies of your children or students?

_____
_____
_____
_____
_____
_____
_____
_____

**CHAPTER TWO**

# RELATIONSHIP-BUILDING WORDS

When we first come into the world, crying is our primary mode of communication. In a few months, babies will start putting together their first words. The average toddler's vocabulary is between fifty and one hundred words. When we are young, words help us make sense of the world. We also use words to form relationships. It's the same for adults. Our vocabulary and ability to communicate with tone and body language grow by leaps and bounds, but we still use words for the same reason.

One of the critical factors in determining a child's future success is whether they have stable, committed, and healthy relationships with adults in their lives. Rudasill (2011) examines a wide range of studies that show that the quality of these relationships affects children's language development, behavior, interaction with peers, and school adjustment. Children benefit from responsive relationships with adults in two ways: they promote healthy brain development and provide the buffering protection required to prevent challenging experiences from producing a toxic stress response (Cohen, 2017). Our words influence our relationships with children, whether we are their parents, guardians, mentors, or teachers. Webster defines relationships as "the way two or more people regard and treat each other." (Merriam-Webster's Collegiate, 2019) Even through their daily interactions with adults, children are learning how to treat others and be in positive relationships with them. It starts early with our "serve and return" interactions with young children. When an infant or young child babbles, gestures, or cries, and an adult responds appropriately with eye contact, words, or a hug, neural connections are built and strengthened in the child's brain that supports the development of communication and social skills. Neuroscientists can now demonstrate how the brain reacts to early language exposure. Conversational interactions can have a visible benefit on brain development, according to one study led by Rachel Romeo, a neuroscientist and speech-language pathologist at Boston Children's Hospital (Romeo, et al. 2018). The researchers taped conversations in families' homes, noting the language they were exposed to and the number of conversational turns. Children who participated in more turn-taking conversations performed better on language comprehension tests. In addition to language development, children need to see adults who can be patient and provide support, encouragement, coaching, and show that they care about them.

For several years, I taught middle school health education. Many of my students loathed this semester, not because they hated my health class but because it was the semester that they did not get to take physical education. What made it even worse was that my classroom was adjacent to the gymnasium. Imagine trying to learn mental health strategies or the food pyramid while hearing balls bouncing and winning screams from the other side of the wall. While I was never a fan of this scheduling choice, I understood the connection between physical education and health education.

Devon, one of my seventh-grade students, would walk into class every day and ask, "Can I just go to the gym? Why do I have to be here?" He complained and whined daily about what he viewed as his nine-week sentence. Even though it was frustrating, and I frequently wanted to scream, "Stop asking me that!" I responded, "I'm sorry, but I am glad you are here." All students want, need, and deserve to be valued and respected—as individuals and as part of a group. This is true even when their behavior is less than ideal. It took me a while to realize this, but I now believe the children who need love the most will often ask for it in the most unloving ways. I responded calmly and respectfully to Devon, and I was intentional about not engaging in a power struggle. I didn't take his complaint personally and acknowledged his desire to play a good volleyball game rather than learn the difference between proteins and carbohydrates. Eventually, his complaints stopped, and I believe it was primarily due to how I interacted with him.

Devon did not have to take health education the following year, but he appeared in my classroom weekly. He'd walked in the same way he had the year before, but his question was different this time. He asked, "Can I come back to your class?" The same young man who complained about disliking health education asked to return. I don't think it was because Devon needed a refresher on mindfulness strategies or how to eat healthily, it was because of the relationship formed in my class.

I have heard stories from teachers who have had students like Devon. Students from previous years who maintain contact with you and relish the memories of their time in classes. Great teachers build students' academic knowledge and cognitive capacity and form positive relationships. Like Devon, we have made an impression on them, and they remember it. They may have been your model student, or they may have been the one who initially was just a little difficult to like (yes, there are some), but they return to say hello, check in, and let you know how they are doing. They remember that you cared about more than just their grade or the subject you were teaching; you cared about them as a person. A positive relationship was formed, and their feelings can shift from "Why do I have to be here?" to "Can I come back to your class?"

In K-12 classrooms, teachers form relationships with their students through everyday interactions. Relationships are the positive connections between students, adults, and peers that foster positive social interaction and establish a nurturing environment of trust and support in schools. Some educators dismiss the importance of relationships in schools because they sometimes seem too "touchy-feely." They mistakenly believe relationships are only about raising students' self-esteem when they need to raise achievement levels. But relationships are not just to feel good but are essential in working toward a common goal of student achievement. Author and researcher Dr. Zaretta Hammond asserts, "Relationships are the onramp to learning, and this statement is supported by science. When we feel cared for, our brains are filled with neurotransmitters and hormones like oxytocin. The same hormone makes moms fall in love with their babies after the pain and work of labor. These "happy chemicals" tell the prefrontal cortex (the thinking part of our brain) that we are safe on a social, emotional, and physical level. Then all systems go for learning." To help children and prime their brains for learning, we can incorporate the five A's into our relationship building:

### Five A's - Acceptance, Attention, Affection, Affirmation, and Appreciation

*Acceptance* means communicating that it is all right for the child to be as they are regardless of culture, ability, or personal style. We do not need to pretend that whatever a child does is correct, but we should always indicate that children have dignity and are worthy of care.

***Attention*** means making yourself available to children by sharing time and energy with them. Parents make time to interact with and listen to their children. Teachers pay attention to students by greeting them by name and demonstrating genuine interest in their lives outside school. Words of attention remind children that they are essential. It says, "I see you," and "You're important to me." When kids receive regular doses of healthy, positive attention, they feel cared for and do not need to seek attention though negative behaviors. In addition, words of attention remind children that they are not facing their challenges alone.

***Affection*** means "I like you." Parents can never tell children "I love you" too much. However, it can be difficult for adolescents to accept or demonstrate affection with their adults. They are easily embarrassed, and some would choose death over letting their friends see their mother kiss them goodbye or responding with an "I love you too" at drop off. Teens still need the validation that comes from their parents' love during periods in their lives when they struggle with low levels of self-confidence, and their peers make fun of them for the smallest things. Teens may prefer to receive text messages with the "I love you" reminder. Educators show affection by telling students, "I like having you in my class." This human connection is critical in all relationships.

***Affirmation*** means making positive statements about children that recognize desirable traits or virtues, such as courage, cheerfulness, dedication, enthusiasm, friendliness, or helpfulness. Virtues Language™ can be used to affirm children using a three-part model statement that contains 1) an opening phrase, 2) a virtue, and 3) how the virtue is being shown or needs to be shown. "I acknowledge your determination to complete this task without giving up," or "I honor your reliability in being here on time every day." Affirming children's uniqueness and helping them recognize their own value makes them more likely to act with compassion and honesty and gives them a greater sense of self-worth.

***Appreciation*** means showing children we are proud of their accomplishments and pleased with their behavior. We give them compliments, express our gratitude, and describe how they contributed positively. Appreciation can be expressed verbally, in writing, electronically, or through actions toward others. When expressing appreciation, it is essential to focus on the deed rather than the doer. The language of appreciation can also include three parts: 1) the action, 2) how we feel about it, and 3) the action's positive effect. For example, a teacher might say, "David, when you complete your assignment as you did today, I feel very pleased because we can get all our work done on time."

Our words help to build strong children and foster strong relationships. Consider these five A's of positive relationships that reflect the words of those who care and want the best for children (Albert, 2012, p.115). Hopefully, there are episodes in your childhood memories where you can remember getting the five A's from parents or adults who understood the power of words. These are examples of language that demonstrates the five A's:

**Words of Acceptance**
"You matter."
"You're okay."
"I see you."

**Words of Attention**
"It's good to see you."
"I notice you have…"
"I remember when you said…"

**Words of Affection**
"I like you."
"I love you." (parents/caregivers)
"You're the best!"

**Words of Affirmation**
"That was thoughtful…"
"That was kind."
"You are a generous person."

**Words of Appreciation**
"Thank you for doing…"
"Thank you for being…"
"This (school, class, soccer team) is better because of you."

I attended the ASCD (Association of Supervision and Curriculum Development) conference in Chicago several years ago when Dr. Maya Angelou was the keynote speaker. I watched in amazement as Dr. Angelou delivered a powerful address to over 10,000 attendees. She began with a song of hope and gratitude: "When it looked like the sun wouldn't shine anymore, God put a rainbow in the cloud." She captivated the entire audience of educators with her gift of using words to remind us of the traumas that some of our students bring to school. Teachers, Maya explained to great applause, are the rainbows in their clouds. She reminded us, "You have enhanced the possibility of seeing light and opportunity in the lives of so many children. I thank you for that." Positive relationships are essential for all children, especially those experiencing life challenges from family transitions, trauma, or even unwelcome class changes. As a result, our words should be thoughtful, intentional, and purposeful.

## Takeaways

- The brain learns through connection. Children learn from their interactions with teachers, coaches, mentors, aunts, uncles, grandparents, and their friends' parents.
- Building strong relationships includes communication that encourages, teaches, and corrects.
- When we feel cared for, our brains are filled with "happy chemicals" that benefit self-esteem and learning.
- Using the five A's can provide support and build young people's self-worth.

## Pause for Reflection

Can you recall your favorite teacher or relative? How do your memories relate to using the five A's in their language?

_____

_____

_____

_____

_____

_____

_____

_____

**CHAPTER THREE**

# OMG!!
## (OPTIMISM, MINDFULNESS, AND GRATITUDE)

Our words are frequently the result of our attitudes about life. They reflect what we are feeling, and thinking and how we approach the world in terms of past, present, and future events. Unsurprisingly, having a positive outlook makes us happier, more successful, and healthier. Maintaining a positive outlook can be difficult, especially in stressful situations; however, learning how to do so, especially around our children, is worthwhile. People with a positive attitude are less vulnerable to chronic stress and may live longer lives. What we say to children matters when it relates to demonstrating mindsets of optimism, mindfulness, and gratitude: OMG!!

## Optimism

Honestly, I am a glass-half-full, rose-colored glasses kind of person. I can see the best in people and look forward to the positive aspects of life. "Glass half full" and "rose-colored glasses" are popular idioms that are often used negatively. I've been told many times that I need to see life for what it really is and not let my rose-colored glasses cloud my view. Optimism is derived from the Latin word "optimum," which means "best." Optimism is not singing a happy tune in the face of adversity or repeating meaningless, hollow words. Optimism is our personal perception and level of hope for the future. It is seeing what's best and focusing and speaking on the positive things we look forward to in our future.

Optimism is a set of beliefs and characteristics that assist individuals in focusing on the positive aspects of life rather than the negative. It's easy to say that focusing on optimism will make someone *feel* better than pessimism and complaining. But there are other benefits from focusing on optimism and using words that encourage it. The book *Learned Optimism: How to Change Your Mind and Your Life*, by Martin Seligman (2006) highlights three advantages of teaching optimism to children:

- It encourages a healthier lifestyle.

- An optimistic outlook is associated with improved academic and extracurricular performance.

- It develops the resilience and strength necessary to make it through challenging times.

While in a high school counseling office, I overheard a conversation between a mom and her teenage daughter as she was registering for Fall classes. Discussing the available courses, her mom said, "Since you enjoy science, you should take Advanced Placement (AP) Biology. It may have a lot of homework, but you will get college credit." The daughter sighed and said, "I heard that class was hard. What if I fail?" Her mother quickly replied to her pessimism and said optimistically, "But what if you pass?"

The opposite of optimism is pessimism. Pessimism can be defined as a focus on the negative aspects of a situation or event and the expectation of a negative outcome. Pessimism is often characterized as "seeing the glass as half empty." Pessimists also complain regularly. According to Will Bowen, author of *The Complaint-Free Relationship,* the average person complains fifteen to thirty times daily (Bowen, 2009).

Responsible adults balance this natural response of complaining and teaching our children not to see the worse in everything. Kids often express their thoughts aloud: "My hair looks ugly" or "I don't have any friends." Some kids use negative words or phrases out of habit. The problem is that negative words can have more power over them the more they hear, read, or say it. Our brain searches for patterns and consistency by learning through repetition.

Help children to arrest and reject their negative thoughts and pessimistic self-talk. Stop and discuss their internal dialogue. Encourage them to police their brains and arrest their ANTs (Automatic Negative Thoughts). We often hear children voice their negative thoughts when faced with challenges or uncertainties. Have you ever heard a child say, "Why bother? I won't make the team anyway," "It doesn't matter. I'm not going to pass," or "I probably won't make any friends." Negative thoughts are also a form of self-handicapping. The language is intended to avoid effort in the hope of avoiding potential implementation failure. Provide children with solid examples of optimistic self-talk. If we are pessimistic about everything from the weather to our schedule to our goal of losing weight, our children will follow our example.

Even at an early age, assisting children in overcoming negative thoughts can go a long way in helping them develop into self-reliant and optimistic adults in the future. In their book, *The Brain Warrior's Way* (2017), Daniel and Tanya Amen remind us that we all have moments when negative thoughts enter our minds. Model and encourage children to challenge negative thoughts by asking these four questions:

- Is it (the negative thought) true?
- Can I absolutely know that it is true?
- How do I react when I think that thought?
- Who would I be without that thought? Or how would I feel if I didn't have that thought?

Simply having a thought does not make it true, nor does it obligate us to entertain it. "Thoughts lie; they lie a lot," the

Amens say, and it is our unquestioned or uninvestigated thoughts that steal our happiness. (Amen & Amen, 2017) It has nothing to do with whether or not a thought is true. We can teach them to be more optimistic through our language. We can do the following 3 things in classrooms and in homes to boost optimism in our children.

- Asking children to first identify all the obstacles in front of them, then decide how they can erase, mitigate, or minimize them.
- Use powerful positive words ("When you pass the class vs. "If you pass the class")
- Set BIG goals to create their future life and MICRO goals for the coming week.

As parents and educators, we can help children form neural pathways with positive words and optimistic thoughts.

## Mindfulness

At the beginning of each school year, I would intentionally speak words of encouragement and great wishes each day before my children went to school. My daughter would leave for the bus, and I would tell her to have an amazing day. As I dropped my son off at school, I would tell him the same. But as the school year progressed and the routine got more set, I noticed my language had changed. Stress got high, schedules tightened, and I heard myself shifting from "Have a wonderful day" to "You better not miss the bus" and "Don't you make me late for work!"

I did not like what I heard, and I did some self-examination. I had allowed our family mornings to turn into times full of hurried and nagging words. I wanted to talk to my kids more intentionally and with more encouragement.

Not to be confused with meditation, mindfulness is about having a non-judgmental sense of awareness about sensations, feelings, and those around you. Mindfulness is the basic human ability to be fully present, aware of where we are and what we're doing, and not overly reactive or overwhelmed by what's happening around us. There are many circumstances we face in which we need to slow down and be thoughtful. Mindfulness is when we shift our minds out of autopilot and intentionally focus on the interaction that is happening in front of us. As a wife, mother, ministry student, and educational consultant, my autopilot sometimes feels like my only survival mode. The fast track of my brain knows when to get up, cook meals, take the kids to school, schedule meetings, teach classes, book business travel, study, contact clients, add kids' activities to my calendar, and still maintain some sense of normalcy.

Young people observe how we deal with frustration, anger, disappointment, and difficulties in our lives and how we express positive emotions such as joy, love, contentment, and peace. How we manage difficult emotions and situations will significantly impact how children react when facing challenges.

One simple and effective practice can help us improve our mindfulness and model how to do the same for children. The practice is to simply... pause.

Pause before speaking and consider how you feel about what is happening. There is power in the pause. Most people have only met a few people in their lives who have listened carefully and responded thoughtfully. When engaging someone in this manner, the conversation frequently slows down as it becomes evident that you are not engaged in a "normal" conversation, that is, the spontaneous and typical back and forth. When one person brings more presence and thoughtfulness to a conversation, the other person will often respond in kind. This is also true for our children. Being present and mindful requires regular practice and support for children and teenagers. Just like learning to play an instrument or ride a bicycle, mindfulness takes intentional practice. Encourage children when eating their meals, when playing with the dog, when visiting with grandparents, when on vacation, to pause, take a deep breath, be present, and experience the moment.

Adults should teach the power of the pause when children are calm. Teachers can make it a part of their classroom conversations and procedures early in the school year. Children will be more focused and calmer and thus more likely to be successful. The brain will have difficulty processing if you attempt to teach or force a pause during a conflict or when tensions are high. I see this happening at many schools that I visit. A student is upset and having a tough time, and an adult is trying to get them to pause and take a breath. "Calm down! Just breathe!" they say. Without prior practice of how to pause and breathe, it is the same as trying to teach a drowning person how to swim. The ability to learn the skill is not the issue. They are not in a proper mindset to learn it quickly at that moment. Even before they master practicing the pause, children do not usually have full-blown meltdowns without warning. Mindful adults notice the first signs of distress and respond to them with words to deescalate and diffuse. They use mindful language.

Instead of
"CALM DOWN!"
You can say
"Take a Deep Breath"

Instead of
"STOP CRYING!"
You can say
"Use your words and Tell me what you need."

Instead of
"STOP YELLING!"
You can say
"Use your inside voice and tell me what happened."

Once we have taught mindful language, a parent of a child who struggles with homework or is overwhelmed after a disagreement with his sibling can be reminded to take a mindful moment.

"I know math frustrates you," you could say. "Math can be a difficult subject, but you can do this. Let's take a moment to grab a sip of water, and then we can get back to the next problem."

"Take a moment and think about how your brother felt when you took his game without asking."

Children can apply the ability to more emotional situations when they understand how to pause. But pausing isn't just for when things aren't going well; pausing helps us to appreciate the moment and even remember it better in the future. Pausing on my busy morning helps me cherish my time with my growing children and to be mindful of sending them off to school with words of encouragement.

Mindful language requires us to think before we speak, pause, and allow ourselves time to decide if what we are about to say is necessary, that it is said from a "healthy" place, and that it is not just said for the sake of saying it. It is an act of profoundly understanding the words we use and learning how these words affect others. In addition, being more mindful has helped me to remember that busy moments with my children today will become my precious memories tomorrow.

## Gratitude

Let me start with a disclaimer: I have an internal bias against ungrateful people. Whenever I meet someone who complains about everything or who can't appreciate the gift of a new day, who can't acknowledge a door held open for them, or a waiter who refills their glass, I silently think to myself, "Wow, someone forgot to teach you to be grateful."

One of my most treasured virtues is gratitude. From an early age, my parents instilled in me the importance of appreciating my many blessings and the things others do for me. My mother used to tell me that not saying thank you did more than just show that I didn't have manners. It was a formal indictment of <u>her</u> parenting skills. If I didn't demonstrate gratitude for a gift or compliment, I would hear about it soon, if not immediately.

"Morgan, I am so grateful that you are a part of this family." The first time I explicitly said this to my daughter, she was about ten years old, and she looked at me with eyes of surprise and awe. Even though I have always felt it, I intentionally expressed to her how grateful I was to be her mom. My daughter is creative, considerate, talented, and hardworking, and I want her to know how grateful I am to be her mom. Even if it feels awkward at first, or if they show a confused or cynical expression as she did when I said it, the message is essential and will stick with them.

Gratitude can be considered an emotion, a virtue, a moral sentiment, a motive, a coping response, a skill, or an attitude. It is all of these and more. Gratitude is that voice that reminds us to be thankful even when we are feeling sorry for ourselves.

We are grateful for our health, family, and a roof over our heads. Gratitude involves being thankful and appreciative, which has been linked to several mental and physical health benefits. When the brain focuses on gratitude, the neurotransmitter serotonin is released. Serotonin is a feel-good chemical that enhances the brain's alertness and can create a more optimal position for our brain to learn.

Many children do not appreciate what they have. It's not their fault. According to Dr. Paul Eckman, an emotions researcher and psychologist, gratitude is not a hard-wired human emotion. He suggests none of us are born grateful. Gratitude must be taught or modeled before it can be expressed. Unfortunately, it might be easier to become a complainer without intentional teaching and guidance. In American culture, we pride ourselves in teaching our children to become independent, which is a vital skill. Children need to learn how to trust themselves, make good choices, and solve problems independently. Sometimes, however, this emphasis on independence can begin to eat away at the importance of gratitude. Gratitude is about looking outside of yourself, and I think that when children are taught to be overly independent, they can easily miss out on the blessings and gifts that are all around them. When adults decide to have an attitude of gratitude, it inspires children to do the same.

Andrea Hussong, director of the Center for Developmental Science at UNC-Chapel Hill, encourages us to nurture these four elements in children to help them experience gratitude (2019):

- NOTICE what is in their lives for which they can be grateful.
- THINK about why they have been given those things.
- Consider how they FEEL about the things they have been given.
- What they can DO to express appreciation in return.

Even children who live in impoverished areas or have been through traumatic experiences can often identify for whom or what they are grateful. Family, friends, a place to live, or friends to hang out with are all examples. Gratitude practices are not intended to minimize any difficulties students may face. According to Bryan Harris, author of *17 Things Resilient Teachers Do*: and *4 Things They Hardly Ever Do*, "Gratitude isn't about ignoring the challenges in life; it's about recognizing the blessings." (Harris, 2020). It focuses on what's good in our lives and being thankful.

## OMG!! (Optimism, Mindfulness, and Gratitude)

Over the last few years, I've received at least 50 emails from former workshop participants who have shared comments and photos of the children's responses to a "what I am grateful for" activity. The majority have come from educators conducting gratitude activities with their students. Although some teachers reported that their children were grateful for their iPads and toys, most teachers were pleasantly surprised to learn that most children were grateful for many of the same things as adults. One teacher at a Baltimore area school sent me copies of her classes' "I am grateful..." notes her students wrote:

> ...*my father is returning home this weekend after his deployment.*
> ...*that my grandmother is out of the hospital.*
> ...*for my sister, even though I make her mad sometimes.*
> ...*that the food pantry is open.*
> ...*for you (the teacher).*

Have children think back over their past week and write down five things they were grateful for in their life. Then "Run the Credits" and give children time to acknowledge others that have helped them. For example, a teacher could model by stating, "Ms. Nickelson took time out of her busy schedule to help me put together an amazing science lab! She saved me a

HUGE amount of time, and I am grateful for her!" A parent could model by stating, "Morgan, you set the table for dinner, which helped the family eat sooner. I am grateful for your help." Parents can have children use a card or shoe box to create a gratitude box. Have them take five minutes to write down three to five things they are grateful for on an index card or piece of paper and place it in the box at the end of each week. Challenge them to think for one minute about what they will write before they start writing and to be as specific as possible.

As a parent, we should be aware of what our children are grateful for and how we can continue to highlight how fortunate they are, knowing that being fortunate entails more than just having material possessions. I'm not saying we should demand that our children be grateful because it doesn't happen that way, but we can examine how we display gratitude in front of them. Express gratitude to the store clerk who helps, wave in the rearview mirror when a fellow motorist allows us to merge, or express gratitude when our spouse/loved one cooks or buys dinner.

Teachers can intentionally foster a more genuine exploration of gratitude by going beyond asking children for whom or what they're grateful. It's also essential to help children consider **why** someone has done something for them, the cost, and the benefits they received from the act. Children also can become more grateful by identifying people who appreciate them for who they are, consider what they need, and choose to do something nice for them.

## Takeaways

- OMG words—optimism, mindfulness, and gratitude—help to create a positive outlook for adults and children.
- Provide children with a strong example of optimism through positive self-talk. Teach children how to have a positive expectation of good things.
- Help children make positive predictions about their lives, families, or the world. This activity can also lead

to a sense of optimism connected to having a positive view of your future.

- Mindfulness in language means we pay attention to our words. We are intentional about what we say and how we say it.

- Create physical reminders or incorporate prompting questions to remind children of the many things for which they can be grateful.

- We want children to naturally begin to see their own lives through an appreciative lens as they witness us demonstrating gratitude.

## Pause for Reflection

How will you prompt words/feelings of optimism, mindfulness, and gratitude in your children or students?

_____
_____
_____
_____
_____
_____
_____

## CHAPTER FOUR

# LABEL PRODUCTS, NOT CHILDREN

I was the principal of an elementary school when I met five-year-old Carter. Having only taught grades 5-12, learning how to understand and connect with elementary-age children was new. One day, I learned the impact of a label on a child. Carter had been sent to my office after throwing toys during circle time. After pausing to calm him, I asked Carter what had happened. "I'm a bad boy, and that's what bad boys do!"

> *His response surprised me.*
> *"Who said you were a bad boy?" I inquired.*
> *"My mommy," he said innocently and childishly.*

I was stunned, and my heart dropped. This "frozen moment" reminded me of the impact of adults' words. Children hear and internalize everything that is said to and about them. This five-year-old was repeating what he had heard from his mother, a woman I am sure loved him but gave him a label at some point, which would not serve him well.

Labels are a part of our world; they help us differentiate one thing from another, which isn't always bad. On the other hand, labels can hinder educational development when they are used to dismiss, insult, or divide intelligence. Too often, negative labels have harmed, needlessly limited, or diminished young lives. Some children are labeled "difficult" or " bad" because of their behaviors. The problem with this language is that these words imply something is wrong with the child. As if the child's behavior is both the problem and the reason we're having trouble with them. Adults and children can and will make poor choices, but our choices do not define us. We can

## Label Products, Not Children

all demonstrate behaviors that can define us at any moment but not for a lifetime. Instead of saying things like, "You are shy," or "Don't be shy," try saying things like, "It takes a little while for you to feel comfortable with new people," or "You are talkative with people you know well." By labeling a child "difficult," we turn their behavior into a part of their personality. When this happens, it's easy to lose hope, give up, and think that this child can't grow or get better. In addition, negative labels can become self-fulfilling prophecies. Children who hear adults refer to them as lazy, dumb, or slow can begin to accept these words as truth. Thus, labels can affect their attitudes toward school, their behavior, and their level of academic and social success.

"Carter, you are not bad. You are a wonderful, smart little boy," I assured him. "What you did was not good, but *you* are not bad. Now, let's plan how you will clean up your mess and apologize to your class and teacher." Later that day, before leaving to go home, Carter saw me in the hallway and ran and hugged me tightly. Although many kindergarteners are affectionate, I hope Carter's hug proved that he heard and understood what I said that day.

Most parents and educators want to help children be their best, but when children's behaviors overwhelm us, our first emotional response can often be annoyance or frustration. When we feel overwhelmed by our student's behavior, we seek explanations to help us comprehend why they are acting in such a manner. We believe the reasoning will help us understand and lead us to a more effective response. This is how students often get labels. *Fostering Resilient Learners* author Kristen Souers asks, "Do we believe that a student needs a diagnosis to describe his or her behavior, or does that diagnosis fulfill our own need to attribute the behavior to a particular cause?" (Souers & Hall, 2016)

In schools, labeling is a deeply complicated issue with many layers. Labels assigned to children can impact the formation and development of students' identities or self-concepts—how they see and define themselves and interact with others. Labels play a significant role in academic discussions. Educators may use labels such as "struggling readers," "ELL students," "gifted students," and "special education students" to define and identify the needs of their students. Labels are typically determined by specific testing or identifiers, and they are assigned to students to assist them in obtaining the assistance they require to be successful. The unnecessary labeling of children with special needs is called disability labeling. It can profoundly affect the self-esteem of children who require just a little more attention than others to learn certain concepts.

We limit children when we reduce them to a single behavior or category. We cut down the complexity of who they were created to be and minimize their potential for growth or change. Our abilities are constantly changing. What does it mean to be a struggling reader? What can get translated is 'you are not as good,' which impacts our mindset. That's where the danger lies.

As adults, we would resent our bosses or partners referring to us using the labels we often use for children. Imagine hearing your spouse tell you or someone else that you were lazy with low abilities or your boss telling you to sit in the front due to your hyperactive tendencies. I often hear from adults in my workshops that they still remember the labels used for them as children growing up. Often, they speak of the resentment that they still feel because of them. Labels such as "the good/bad twin," "lazy," "nerd," or even "smarty-pants." Labels can be difficult to remove, yet it is never too late to change and become aware of the harmful effects of labels or to work to reframe a negative behavior. Consider the potential label's cost and how it will affect children now and in the future.

Consider your actions, personality, or behaviors as a child. Have you grown and changed since elementary or middle school? Brain research and common sense would dictate that you have, although personality science suggests that there are probably some consistencies since your early years. Even if some behaviors continue, as we grow, we learn to "follow the rules" and adjust our behavior accordingly. In my case, it was talking more than the teachers would have liked, and if I am honest, my husband might still complain of the same behavior today. Ms. Wilkens saw me as a good communicator and not just talkative. Her reframing helped her to help me positively use my voice and learn when to "push pause" on my talking. Today, perhaps because of Ms. Wilkin's actions and mindset, I can say that I have never been dismissed from a staff meeting or reprimanded in a movie theater for talking too much.

As we seek to reframe children's behaviors, even those that initially have negative connotations can be reframed into more positive ones. Instead of referring to a child as "bossy," try saying a child with "leadership potential," or instead of calling the child "hyperactive," try "energetic." Instead of referring to a child as "stubborn," try to say "determined." The author of *The Heart of Education*, Dara Feldman, says we can leverage a student's strength by acknowledging the underlying virtue that is represented. (2013) The virtue of determination is celebrated when saying to the "stubborn child," "Wow! I noticed that you never give up. You have such determination."

Removing harmful labels entails much more than simply changing a word. Harmful labels convey a negative societal message that creates assumptions about children and what they are incapable of doing. They can have an impact and limit a child's potential. Negative labels can cause adults and even other children to expect the worst of a child. Negative messages will continue to impact vulnerable children in our homes and schools without deliberate actions to change how labels are used.

## Takeaways

- Labels assigned to children by adults can impact the formation and development of children's identities.
- Describe behavior. Don't label it.
- If our mindset dictates that "problem children" will always cause problems, our words will deflate children with labels.
- Reframing negative labels and behaviors can help us see the strength or virtue of the behavior.

## Pause for Reflection

Did you have a label assigned to you as a child? Do you remember another child who was referred to as the "_____" child? What impact did that have on you or how you interacted with them?

_____
_____
_____
_____
_____
_____
_____
_____

**CHAPTER FIVE**

# WHAT WE SPEAK STARTS IN OUR MIND

Author and researcher Carol Dweck (2007) made known the terms "Fixed and Growth Mindset." Dweck's research demonstrates the power of our most fundamental beliefs. Much of what we believe we know about ourselves and others stems from our "mindset." Our way of thinking becomes a habit. Many of our thoughts are repetitive; therefore, the chances are high that you'll have the same thoughts today that you had yesterday. If we do something often enough, our brain creates a neural pathway. The more we do it, the stronger the connections in the brain become. Our mindsets are habits, like footprints in the sand. Our mindset both propels us and keeps us from reaching our full potential. They can also impact our belief the in the potential of others. An adult with a fixed mindset limits a child's potential to their current level of functioning. An adult with a growth mindset embraces the belief and the conviction that children grow and change. Research demonstrates that we can shift a child's mindset from fixed to growth, resulting in increased motivation and achievement. In a 2012 TED talk, Carol Dweck suggested that educators have a critical role in fostering a growth mindset in children, including their language and actions. "Growth mindset is about embodying it in all the everyday practices that educators do. Presenting material with students' understanding that you think they can all learn it to a high level. It's collaborating with students and giving feedback on their learning processes. It's about helping children relish challenges because they can help them grow their abilities."

*What We Speak Starts in Our Mind*

## FIXED MINDSET AND GROWTH MINDSET

| FIXED MINDSET | GROWTH MINDSET |
|---|---|
| "Failure is the limit of my abilities" | "Failure is an opportunity to learn" |
| "I don't like to be challenged" | "Challenges help me grow" |
| "I'm either good at it or I'm not. I can either do it or not" | "My effort and attitude determine my abilities" |
| "Feedback and criticism are personal" | "Feedback is necessary and constructive" |
| "My potential is predetermined" | "I can learn to do anything I want" |
| "When I'm frustrated, I give up" | "I'm inspired by the success of others" |
| "I shy away from uncertainty and stick to what I know" | "I embrace uncertainty and try new things" |

Create language for a growth mindset. "Yes, this is hard, but I can do hard things." When children become discouraged or hesitant, remind them, "You've got what it takes. I know you, and you're a hard worker who never gives up." A growth mindset is about learning how to fail well and knowing that learning from failure leads to eventual success. This can be summed up in the sentence, "I can't do that… YET." A growth mindset utilizes the power of yet. "Yet" implies that something is achievable. By framing low grades or mistakes as an opportunity to improve, instead of a final result, we provide children with the confidence to continue learning. "Yet" provides a path forward. Parents often ask children, "How was your day?" or "What did you learn at school?" If they are anything like my children, they will give a general answer like "It was okay" or "Nothing." Use reflective questions to promote a growth mindset and foster better communication.

Sample Growth Mindset Questions

- What strategy did you try?
- How will you challenge yourself today?
- Did you ask for help if you needed it?
- What can you learn from this experience?
- What's one mistake you made today? How can you learn from it?

*Check out musician Janelle Monae as she performs "The Power of Yet" on one of my favorite children's programs, Sesame Street, and explains how useful the word "yet" can be. https://www.youtube.com/watch?v=XLeUvZvuvAs*

Cliches such as "a tiger can't change its stripes" or "you can't teach an old dog new tricks" should only be used when speaking of animals. Some adults mistakenly apply these beliefs or mindsets to a child's learning ability. A child who struggles in math may not always struggle at math; think Thomas Edison. A child who doesn't play basketball well may grow to become a famous basketball icon; think Michael Jordan. A child who stutters or barely speaks may become a world-renowned author, poet, and speaker, think Maya Angelou. Avoid limiting words such as "I wasn't good at math, so my son will probably fail math too." The mindset reflected is that children do not grow or change and most of us consciously know this is not true. The road to competence is paved with setbacks and hiccups, but we can help children navigate these moments. The language we use significantly impacts children's mindsets about their abilities. Great parents and teachers must be intentional to ensure that their words and actions reflect the belief that children have the potential to do more than even their current level of performance or behavior dictates.

I was talkative in school as a child. I talked to my neighbors in class and often got into trouble for constant chatter. I am sure my teachers would have labeled me most likely never to stop talking. Ironically, I believe being talkative is a common trait for those who pursue careers in education. Teachers get to talk a lot; sometimes we, too, can talk too much. In school, my teacher's comments on my report cards often read, "Shauna will do better if she learns to stop talking," or "Shauna's talking keeps her from staying focused." My parents were called. I was kept inside during recess and even had tape placed over my mouth to punish me for my talkative behavior. (Never do this.) My mother would scold me, punish me, and remove some privileges. I would do better, but only for a brief time.

Many of my teachers in elementary and middle school could not see beyond my annoying behavior and struggled with how to stop it. Even today, many teachers admit that learning how to deal with behavior, especially challenging behavior, was not a part of their education and they thus feel overwhelmed by trying to determine how to address misbehavior (Greene, 2008). However, I was fortunate to have a teacher who could reframe my behavior and see my potential. Her name was Ms. Wilkins, and she was my eleventh-grade accounting teacher. She didn't try to dismiss me, and she didn't let my chatty behavior overwhelm her. She did something that demonstrated that she saw beyond my behavior and recognized that I had a strength.

Accounting was an elective class that I did not like. I was just trying to pass. While I liked Ms. Wilkins as a teacher, I had no interest in assets, liabilities, or balance sheets. Several of my friends were in this class, meaning I had plenty of people to talk to. I am sure my incessant conversations were distracting not just to her but to the class.

One day, Ms. Wilkins summoned me to her desk. As I slowly walked to her desk, I had my head down as I expected to be reprimanded for my talking. "Ms. Loquacious," she said, "come meet with me during lunch." Not familiar with the word, I politely corrected her and told her that my name was not Loquacious but that it was Shauna. She gave a bright grin before responding, "Yes. It sure is. Shauna, I'll see you at lunch." During lunch, instead of lecturing me or calling my parents, she took a different approach that forever changed how I saw myself. "Shauna, you have such a unique and beautiful voice," she said. "There is a warmth to it that makes people want to listen to you. That is a gift. Let's help you to get better at not wasting it."

I wasn't sure if she was joking because no one had ever said anything like this to me. Her actions, however, demonstrated that she was sincere in her desire to assist me and see me grow as a communicator. She extended an invitation for me to become a member of an after-school Toastmasters club to hone my public speaking abilities. Toastmasters International is a nonprofit educational organization that teaches public speaking and has helped people from diverse backgrounds become more confident speakers, communicators, and leaders. I was astounded and humbled by her investment in me.

But did it change my behavior in class? Did I continue to be a disruption, or was there a shift in my behavior? Absolutely there was a change. Ms. Wilkins believed in me and invested in me, so I respected her when she occasionally had to remind me, Ms. Shauna, don't waste your words, only use them when you have the floor, and everyone is listening." I immediately complied with her request. She was the first teacher who, without threatening to contact my parents, was successful in getting me to reduce my amount of off-task talking. Her ability to reframe my behavior as a strength has assisted me in gaining a new perspective on the behavior that everyone else considered an annoyance or a defect that required fixing.

A few months later, Ms. Wilkins equipped me to serve as the mistress of ceremony for an end-of-the-year student awards ceremony. What a great honor it was for me to stand before over one thousand of my peers and use my speaking skills positively. The student, often placed in the front or the corner for talking too much, was now center stage using her "gift." Ms. Wilkins' ability to see past my talkative behavior and allow me to stretch and grow my skills has benefited me and my career as an educator and public speaker. I will be forever grateful for her belief in me.

Children are learning and growing every day. Our language should reflect our belief in lifelong learning and development. As a teacher, I sometimes struggled not to limit my students based on my perception of their behavior or current level of performance. Often, it was silly behaviors such as nonstop talking or class clown antics that gave me headaches and led me to limit their ability to do better. In retrospect, I should have known better. Some of my teachers did the same thing to me in school, and I think I have turned out well.

Educators giving students feedback can also reinforce or mitigate a given mindset. Constructive feedback is a powerful tool for academic and social development, and growth in this area requires both praise and criticism. Research conducted by Cohen and David Yegar (2018) investigated how teachers could convey constructive feedback in a way that would lead to student improvement without undermining students' motivation. The researchers helped rephrase teachers' criticism into "wise feedback," which expressed faith in their students' abilities rather than simply a statement that the students were falling short. Wise feedback incorporates three steps:

> STEP 1: Communicate high expectations.
>
> STEP 2: Explain that you believe the student can meet the expectations.
>
> STEP 3: Provide actionable feedback that demonstrates support.

*"Math can seem hard, and this course is challenging. I believe that you can be successful in math. When you learn something, your brain grows as you practice. At the beginning of the problem, there's a missing sign. Go back and include this sign and see how that changes the final value."*

It is critical to communicate high expectations to children and provide them with the support they need to meet them. When children are challenged, they can thrive. However, they must understand the expectations, know how to meet them, and feel that the adult believes in their abilities.

## Takeaways

- Our words reflect our mindset or our beliefs.

- If our mindset embraces children's ability to grow and change, the words we use with them will give them views of limitless possibilities.

- We can use guiding questions to foster a growth mindset in children.

- The beauty of the growth mindset is that it never loses sight of a child's potential.

- Wise feedback sends the message to children: We have high expectations; you will meet them, and we will support you.

## **Moment of Reflection**

Is there something in your past that you think measured you? A test score? A failed relationship? Being fired from a job? Being rejected? Focus on that thing. Now put it in a growth-mindset perspective. Look honestly at your role in it but understand that it doesn't define your intelligence, personality, or anything else about you.

What did you (or can you) learn from that experience?

_____
_____
_____
_____
_____
_____
_____
_____
_____
_____

**CHAPTER SIX**

# WORDS CAN HURT

"Sticks and stones will break my bones, but words will never hurt me!!" I was nine when I nervously yet boldly yelled these words at ten-year-old Beverly on the playground in response to her calling me Black and ugly again. She would do this daily, usually during recess when no teachers were present. Because of desegregation orders issued in the 1980s, I was one of only a few African American students in my elementary school. I was bused to a school about 20 miles from my house, but it was in a very different neighborhood than the one I grew up in, which was predominantly African American. In grades 4-6, I was the only Black student in my class. I was just one of the kids for most of my time there. But to Beverly, I was the source of her racist jokes and slurs. Probably a reflection of language she heard at home; she would tell me that I looked like "burnt trash" at every opportunity. In the cafeteria, at recess, and even during class when out of earshot of the teacher. "Words will never hurt me," I said to myself as I listened to her insults and attempted to reduce the pain of humiliation. I wanted to believe that words couldn't cause pain, but they did. I tried to ignore her. I tried to produce responses that ranged from "that hurts my feelings" to "you are ugly too." But at the end of the day, her words hurt. And they hurt to the point of tears.

No matter what skin we wear or how open-minded or accepting we believe ourselves to be, we all have cultural ways of being that we have unintentionally picked up that can cause or perpetuate harm to others. Since childhood, society has instilled the subtle message that some people are more important than others. There is a social hierarchy to follow that ranks people based on characteristics such as race, class, sexuality, and gender. This "order" of things impacts our actions in ways we don't intend, and therefore we all carry prejudices and biases. Our personal biases as parents and educators significantly influence what we teach and do not teach our children.

Biases and stereotypical mindsets can seep into our language in our homes and schools if they are not properly acknowledged and addressed. Most of the time, this happens unconsciously. Many messages are sent to children subtly through adult behavior, such as facial expressions, posture, and body language. The central message of this book is that children see and hear things even when we think they are not looking.

In other cases, it can be more apparent when adults express their prejudices in front of their children. Biased language contains offensive, discriminatory, or hurtful words or phrases. It makes specific individuals or groups feel misunderstood, excluded, or misrepresented. It is often the result of antiquated social norms and historical oppression. Parents may tell their children not to associate with a particular group of individuals based on limited knowledge or an implicit bias. Unfortunately, racism is a family value for some.

Additionally, there are instances in which we have internalized negative attitudes about identity groups because of racism in our personal experiences. This often happens in groups where negative societal attitudes have impacted how people perceive and feel about themselves. Because bias is learned in the context of intimacy—and family relationships are intimate—children may feel a keen sense of loyalty to uphold negative attitudes if they are the attitudes that even one of their parents demonstrates.

Bias can also have an impact on the classroom. This bias occurs when educators only promote teaching materials and ideas from a single point of view, give more attention to male students, or encourage lighter-skinned students to participate while reprimanding or ignoring darker-skinned students. Students may begin to question their dignity or the dignity of others because of such actions. They may wonder, "Am I good or bad? Who else is good or bad?" Bias in language and communication can sow seeds of self-doubt, division, and discord in the minds and actions of children.

Bias can also exist in labeling students who are not native English speakers. English language learners (ELL) are "emergent bilinguals." By learning English, these children become bilingual and can function in their native language and English. When we ignore the bilingualism that these students can and often must develop through schooling in the United States, they perpetuate inequities in the education of these children. That is, they discount these children's home languages and cultural understandings (Garcia et al., 2008).

We must speak up every time we hear children express biased language. Letting one go, then speaking up against the next, sends an inconsistent message: sometimes bias is okay; other times, it isn't. Comments children make, such as, "I don't want to play with her. She walks funny," or "Alex talks funny." Respond with simple, factual answers, such as, "Alex is learning to speak English. That is why he sounds a little different than you." It is a teachable moment. "Stop what you're doing—whatever you're doing—and address it," Soñia Galaviz, a fifth-grade teacher in Nampa, Idaho, shared with the Learning for Justice organization. If Galaviz is teaching a math lesson and hears a student make a biased remark, what does she do? "I say to myself, 'Hold on, let's stop.' The parallelogram lesson can wait. And I go back to all our work during the first two months of school, discussing classroom culture and sharing our own cultural stories. I address it in the moment. I never let it pass. Anytime you let it pass, it's an opportunity missed."

Establishing an educational foundation for demonstrating dignity, respect, and humanity for all is possible and ideal. As our cities and nation become more pluralistic, most children attend school alongside people from various backgrounds. Those who are not, particularly those who live in more segregated areas, should be made aware of the importance of bringing attention to the issue of diversity and equity. It is critical for our children's personal, educational, and social development that they know how to show respect and honor the dignity of others. According to authors Floyd Cobb and John Krownapple in their book, *The Culture of Dignity*, dignity is something all humans are born with, and it should not be able to be taken from anyone (2019). Dignity accepts people as neither inferior nor superior to you and gives others the freedom to express their authentic selves without fear of being negatively judged. Human dignity is the belief that all people have a special value based solely on their humanity. It has nothing to do with their social class, race, gender, religion, abilities, or anything else other than their humanity.

Furthermore, today's workplace is pluralistic. Children need to learn to work with people of different ethnicities, religious beliefs, races, economic or political backgrounds. The ability to interact effectively with others is as important as, if not more important than, any technical skills that our children will require for any career they choose.

Slurs and racist insults like the ones directed at me still happen today. Children often lack historical context and may have limited knowledge of cultures outside their own. However, words that are hate-filled or racist should never be tolerated. Insults and slurs make children feel unsafe, interfere with their ability to connect with others, and are often learned from adults within their sphere of influence. Correction requires us to undertake the critical task of reflecting on and addressing our personal biases. It is rarely easy work and must be done regularly and continuously.

The impact of parent bias on kids shouldn't be underestimated. In one study, researchers had white parents read books depicting racial issues to their preschool-aged children while being videotaped (under the pretense of studying the effects of literature on learning). Racial attitudes in both parents and their children were measured and compared (Pahlke et al., 2012)

Later analyses of the videos revealed that many parents avoided discussing race, even when their children inquired, and took "colorblind" approaches to the issues raised in the book. Instead of mentioning race, they might say, "It's important to be nice to everyone." Though the parents expected their children to absorb their colorblind ideals and hold favorable views of other races, the children's perspectives did not match these expectations, indicating that a colorblind approach does not reduce biased attitudes in children. This suggests that adults shouldn't gloss over differences by saying things such as, "We're all the same inside." Children can see that people are different. Teach them to learn to live and work with a variety of people and to appreciate and respect their differences.

When today's children reach adulthood, people may, unfortunately, behave much like many do today. People will still use labels, insults, and biases to make others feel less than them. Bullies and bigots will continue to exist on the playground and on social media. Because of this evident human tendency towards bad behavior, today's children, some would argue, should learn how to meet the bullies and the bigots head-on. With this attitude, negative behavior does not change but increases, so we must help our children adapt to a world where people speak harshly and act without kindness.

On the other hand, my "rose-colored glasses" are on again, and I suggest people can do better, and they *will* do better. It requires courage to believe kindness can triumph when there seems to be so much evidence that unkindness is with us to stay. Yet we can hold ourselves responsible for our words and behavior while addressing and creating boundaries for unacceptable and offensive language from others.

Our combined work as parents and educators is to do our part in teaching our children about acceptance, dignity, and the humanity of all people. When we model dignity in our actions and language, we recognize everyone's right to be seen, heard, listened to, and treated fairly. Everyone has the right to feel safe in the world. This means we must be willing to live and model our desired values ourselves. Biases are built on myths and beliefs that are not always supported by evidence or direct experience. For example, there is a general perception that girls talk more in class than boys. In one of their studies, Sadker and Sadker (1985) showed a video clip of a classroom discussion and asked teachers and administrators which gender talked more. Even though quantitative data indicated that boys talked three times as much as girls, most teachers claimed that girls talked more than boys. Acknowledging our own bias is a starting point. After we acknowledge it, we must be vigilant and ensure our language is respectful and upholds dignity and honor.

## Takeaways

- Teach children that words can hurt. Children need to know that hurtful words are unacceptable.

- Biases and stereotypical mindsets can seep into our language in our homes and schools if they are not properly acknowledged and addressed.

- Parents and educators need to talk explicitly about race and the effects of racism.

- It is crucial for our kids' personal, educational, and social growth that they know how to treat their peers with dignity and respect.

- Be sure children see you respond to insensitivity or bias when it occurs. They will feel safe and respected if they know you will not tolerate such behavior.

- Be a role model. Children will start to model your behavior when you treat everyone with respect and consideration.

## Pause for Reflection

How comfortable am I having conversations with children about bias and race? How have I investigated the impact of any biases I may have?

_____

_____

_____

_____

_____

_____

_____

_____

_____

## Going Deeper: Personal Bias Reflection Exercise

The organization, Learning for Justice, provides guiding statements to help explore our experiences with attitudes about difference.

1. The first time I became aware of differences was when...
2. As I was growing up, my parent(s) taught me that people who were different from us were...
3. As I was growing up, my parent(s) taught me that people like us were...
4. A time I was mistreated because of my difference was when...
5. A time I mistreated someone for being different was when...
6. I feel most comfortable when I am around people who...
7. I feel least comfortable when I am around people who...
8. The memories I have of differences affect my parenting by...

(Beyond the Golden Rule: A Parent's Guide to Preventing and Responding to Prejudice, Learning for Justice, 2020)

## CHAPTER SEVEN

# CONFIDENCE BUILDING WORDS

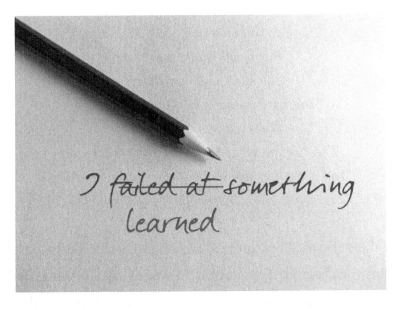

Frustrated by the Chicago Public Schools' low standards, educator Marva Collins withdrew five thousand dollars from her pension, renovated the second floor of her own home, stocked it with secondhand desks and books, and launched the Westside Preparatory School. She worked tirelessly with the "forgotten" children of Chicago's inner city, many of whom could not read and had been labeled "learning disabled" or "uneducable" or had been "written off as losers." She believed these children could learn at high levels and at an accelerated pace. Collins used inspiring and memorable phrases to encourage her students' daily motivation and confidence. Popular mantras Marva Collins taught included:

> *"Success does not come to you;*
> *you must come to it."*
> *"If you can't make a mistake,*
> *you can't make anything."*
> *"You have the right to choose what kind*
> *of person you want to be."*
> *"I realize this is my life to use or throw away."*
> *"You are not in school for your parents, teachers,*
> *or anyone else. You're only here for yourself."*

Collins also used her words to encourage her students to think. She would ask questions such as, "Do you think The Little Red Hen was right not to share her food with the other animals?" "Why was she right?" and "Did the witches make Macbeth do evil?" Her students shared their perspectives on justice and free will based on their own experiences and became comfortable debating with one another. They learned how to think, not what to think, and how to back up their opinions with evidence from the text and their own lives. She fostered student agency by teaching students to value the learning process, not just the content. At the end of the first year, every student scored much higher on standardized test (Biondi, 2018). Her students went from hating school to loving it and gained self-confidence in their abilities.

The word confidence is derived from Latin, which means "with trust," "with faith," or "with belief." Confident children believe in their abilities. Educators and parents want children who believe in themselves. A child's belief in themselves develops over time but often starts with an adult's belief in them. Marva Collins is an amazing example of someone who believed in children, and her actions led her students to develop confidence in themselves. Oprah Winfrey's grandmother is another fitting example of such a person. Oprah Winfrey is an American talk show host, television producer, actress, and author who has spoken publicly about her experiences growing up in poverty and experiencing trauma. Oprah's grandmother saw early on that she had a passion and skill for public speaking and encouraged it. More importantly, Oprah's grandmother supported her and helped her cultivate positive self-esteem, which motivated her to succeed. She believed in Oprah, which allowed Oprah to believe in herself.

If you are a teacher or parent of a young child or a teenager, it is essential to know that children's brains develop in spurts called critical periods. The first occurs around the age of two, and the second during adolescence. The number of connections (synapses) between brain cells (neurons) doubles at the start of these periods. Two-year-olds have twice as many synapses as adults. Because it is through these connections between brain cells that learning occurs, the brain can learn twice as fast as it can at any other time in life. As a result, children's experiences during this stage have a long-term impact on their confidence and development. The language that adults use can also promote or add to modeling resilience. When we encourage them to try new things, even if they fail, we send a message that they are wise and capable of learning from every experience. When a child shares a problem they are facing with a friend, we risk minimizing the situation when we respond, "It's not that bad." Instead, we want children to understand that their problem is real, that they will be able to deal with it, and that we will support them. Likewise, teachers can make it clear that we intend to stick with students during the learning process. When we call on a student for an answer, we work with them until they formulate the answer, even if they get it wrong the first time. This action sends the message, "I am not giving up on you." We should demonstrate our confidence in them as they continue to try, even following a mistake.

Imagine a teacher greeting fifth-grade students first thing in the morning. She starts the day with the following comments:

> *"Come in and get started on your work for today. You should already know what to do. We only have two more days until your opinion paper deadline, which will count as a test grade. I will not accept late work since you have had plenty of time to finish it. Some of you have been playing around, and your grade will reflect that. I've seen your drafts; some of you have a lot of work to do. Now stop talking and get to work."*

The fifth-grade teacher in the next class, who has the same message, begins her class like this:

> "It is wonderful to see all of you on this beautiful morning. Today, you will continue working on your opinion papers. They will look better and more complete as you refine them. Before you is a wonderful opportunity to express your point of view and demonstrate how far you've come in developing your writing skills. I will return the drafts you gave me yesterday with feedback about sentences you can review and rewrite to make them more effective. Are we all looking forward to what we can accomplish today? I know I am!"

The teacher in both examples may have the same goal for the students, yet the words convey a different message. I would love to have my child in the second teacher's class, and as a student, I would have positive feelings about learning in this teacher's class. Sandwiched between her mention of opportunity and the question about looking forward to working on essays, there is a mention of feedback and improving their writing.

Words that set the atmosphere of expectation can build confidence and provide motivation. Now, consider the following words or phrases. Imagine yourself as a child, and listen from their perspective:

> "Your basketball skills are getting better, but why did you let all of those kids score on you at the end? Sometimes I wonder where your mind has gone."
>
> "You showed great progress on this last writing assignment, but your handwriting is horrible. Next time, I will not accept it unless it's neat."
>
> "Although you are good at math, you have a long way to go before you are as sharp as your older brother."

Did the feelings in your mind and body shift? Would you feel motivated to work hard? We can unknowingly discourage children even when we believe we are encouraging them. Even when we are not aware of it, our words have the potential to arouse children's anxieties and fears of impending failure. Sometimes, even well-meaning adults provide a level of encouragement but then compare children to others or insinuate that immediate perfection is expected.

Children gain understanding and skills at an exponential rate from the moment they are born. They can also gain the confidence to put their newfound abilities to use in various situations. How many children learn to walk, swim, or ride a bike on their first try? None. The road to competence is paved with second chances and often a series of setbacks. Children must learn not to avoid or be intimidated by these speed bumps. They will have times in life when they trip, fall, stumble, and get scars, emotionally and physically. We can use words to instill confidence in children while they are on their learning journey.

Instead of
"IS THIS THE BEST YOU CAN DO?"
You can say,
"I want you to succeed, so let's try again."

Instead of
"LET ME KNOW IF YOU DON'T UNDERSTAND."
You can say,
"I'm here if you have questions."

Instead of
"LET ME HELP YOU WITH THAT."
You can say,
"I believe you can do it."

When my son was two and a half years old, he wasn't meeting the pediatric developmental milestones for language. Matthew was a happy and joyful little boy, but he didn't use as many words or even speak as often as other children. When I learned that children at this age should have a vocabulary of about 200 words, my husband and I decided to contact our local family resource center on the advice of our pediatrician. After a three-hour home visit by the speech therapist and child development specialist, they commented, "Mrs. King, Matthew may not be talking much because you don't require him to. You seem to do all the talking for him." It was tough to hear this feedback as a parent. It seems that my loquacious skills were causing problems again. But at that moment, I swallowed my pride and listened to the feedback from the early childhood expert. Assisting my son in developing confidence in his speaking ability began with my willingness to allow him to do so.

Encourage children to speak up on their own during everyday activities. This can start early when parents and teachers help preschoolers develop their language skills. Allow your children to speak when ordering food at a restaurant, selecting a toy at a store, or discussing homework problems with teachers as they get older. Ask them to express what they want and why they want it in complete sentences so that others can understand them. As children grow, their confidence can become just as important as their ability to perform the skills themselves. To thrive, children must have faith in their abilities while learning resilience in facing difficulties, challenges, or setbacks. Through the experiences of mastery and the ability to bounce back from failure, they can develop a healthy level of self-confidence. Today, I am pleased to report that my son is a high-achieving high school student fluent in English and French.

Imagine this scene. You're giving four-year-old directions on how to wash his hands.

> *"Don't make a mess like you did yesterday,"* you say, intending to instill this daily hygiene habit in him. *"Pay attention, and don't get water all over your clothes."*

While the comment is intended to instill confidence in his ability to wash his hands, it is also a negative assessment of his previous performance. The adult's words provide a warning but lack direction and encouragement. Changing the wording of the comment slightly will allow us to outline the details of hand washing in a teachable manner:

*"Keep your elbows close to the counter, then the splashes will fall into the sink, and you will keep your clothes dry."*

Feedback is described as information used to affirm areas of strength in learning and performance and point to areas needing improvement (Frontier, 2021). Our feedback to children must provide specific, understandable, timely, and actionable information to be most effective. Effective feedback is best at home or school when children can utilize it to guide their next steps to improvement.

The road to competence is paved with successes and setbacks, and children must learn to navigate both. Our words can and should demonstrate high expectations while simultaneously providing encouragement and support. Educators can motivate young minds in schools by creating learning-focused terminology and defining clear learning outcomes. If we intentionally emphasize to children that the goal is to increase learning and not simply complete an assignment or activity, their buy-in will increase. Competence precedes confidence. When students are acknowledged for being good learners and not just good students, they are more open to trying more complex activities. Open-ended questions can be used in specific feedback to prompt learners to reflect. For example, "Julian, your classmates had all eyes on you as you gave your presentation. How do you think you drew everyone's attention?" This question reinforces Julian's excellent presentation skills and invites him to reflect on what he did specifically to help him perform well. We can keep motivation and confidence flowing when prioritizing learning and skill development over grades and test scores. Maintaining an emphasis on learning helps children understand that they are active participants in the learning process.

Instead of
"WHAT GRADE DID YOU GET?"
Parents can ask,
"What did you learn?"

Instead of
"THIS IS WRONG."
Teachers can say,
"Try another way."

The language we use to instill confidence directly impacts academic learning and how we give feedback. Consider this feedback statement below from a parent or teacher about a child's homework:

> *"Your writing is very neat and looks great. Next time, remember to put a space between the full stop and the start of the next sentence."*

Now turn it around and place the correction first, then place the more positive statement last:

> *"Next time, remember to put a space between the full stop and the start of the next sentence. The rest of your writing is very neat and looks great."*

In the first statement, it is easier to forget the positive comment on the neat writing and focus on the negative comment. The second statement, although it has the exact words, will leave the child feeling more confident while being mindful of the gap between the full stop and the following sentence.

## Takeaways

- We can instill confidence in children's learning abilities by providing guidance and positive reinforcement.

- Giving a child the opportunity to speak for themselves is an essential and significant practice.

- Competence includes not only learning new skills but also acknowledging the learning process.

## Pause for Reflection

Have you ever received feedback from someone who helped you feel more confident in your work? What was said that helped you move forward and do better?

_____

_____

_____

_____

_____

_____

_____

_____

**CHAPTER EIGHT**

# GOOD JOB AND OTHER WORDS OF PRAISE

How often do we give a child praise for doing a good job? Do we acknowledge a teenager when they clean their room? Do we praise students who are prepared with their homework? Do we ever make a "big deal" about the student who formed a study group on their own? I'm like many of you who might answer, "But that's what they are supposed to do. Why do I need to praise children for what is expected?" Well, here is why. First, we all like being acknowledged for doing the right thing. Think about how good you feel when you receive a notification saying that your credit score has increased. Credit scores increase when we do "what we are supposed to do" to pay the bills or loans that we promised we would. Even if Equifax didn't verbally say a good job, the score increase represents our kudos.

Why else should we be intentional and purposeful with praise words for children? Praise can boost positive feelings and motivation. Praise feels good. It can encourage children to be more cooperative, persistent, and hardworking. Praise activates the reward area in the brain. The brain's response is like getting a financial reward. Researchers believe that by activating this area, praise improves learning during sleep—a process referred to as encoding. In other words: by praising students, we help them learn and perform better.

As most parents and teachers do, I would regularly praise children with the words "good job" or "well done." While there is nothing harmful about these common phrases, there are many more effective ways to encourage children when they do well. Offering specific details along with the complimentary statement can help to reinforce desired behaviors. Without specificity, a child may not understand why they are being praised. When praise is specific, a child can identify what they did that was worthy of a "good job" from the adult, and the chances of them repeating the behavior increase. It's what we call Behavior-Specific Praise (I don't want to refer to it as B.S. praise, but if the acronym helps you to remember to use it, go for it). Behavior-specific praise teaches children how positive behaviors look and feel. Catch children when they are doing the desired behavior, and don't let the moment pass. When we give children this specific, in-the-moment praise, they are more likely to repeat those positive behaviors.

I watched a mother use behavior-specific praise to encourage her daughter's good posture as she prepared for her competitive ballet classes. "Julianna, you look amazing when you hold your shoulders back," she said. "So straight and beautiful. I wish my posture was that good." Her mother's words of praise likely did more to improve her posture than "stop slouching," which was my default response to my daughter for years. When children see that adults recognize their efforts toward a single goal or how hard they work, they feel more validated in their efforts.

Researchers looked at videos of mothers playing with their one, two, and three-year-old children. The researchers recorded how often and what types of praise each mother gave her child. They paid particular attention to how much praise was about the child's effort, like "good throw," and how much was about the child as a person, like "you're so good at baseball." When the children were seven and eight years old, five years later, the researchers talked to them and asked them about their thoughts. For example, "How much would you like to do math problems that are very easy so you can get a lot of them right?" The study found that toddlers praised for their efforts were more likely to like challenges as older kids than those who heard praise directed at them personally.

"Praise is a powerful tool for educators," according to researchers at Vanderbilt University. "When used effectively in the classroom, it can improve students' social and academic performance and classroom climate." Instead of simply saying, "Great job!" teachers can also be more specific. For an English teacher commenting on a student's work, rather than a B+ on the paper, she can say, "Great job! Your introduction is clear and caught my attention. You also wrote two more paragraphs than last week. I admire how dedicated you are!" The teacher's words offer specific praise, encouragement, and an acknowledgment of progress. So, how much praise should children get from adults? Can you praise children too much? It appears the answer is more about finding a balance. Behavioral scientists have long been focused on the ideal praise-to-criticism ratio. The ideal ratio is 5:1. For every negative comment, there should be at least five positive comments to balance it out. (Cook et al. 2017).

I've heard from teachers that sometimes students don't like praise, but when they are praised, students often act nonchalant or embarrassed. I still contend that if giving specific positive feedback or praise is a normal part of the classroom environment and the teacher does this with all students, it will become a habit and a normal part of the culture. Most students won't feel embarrassed or singled out by it.

## Pause for Reflection

How did your parents and teachers praise you as you were growing up? Did they tell you how "smart" you were, or did they focus on how hard you worked? How do you use word of encouragement and praise for your students or children?

_____
_____
_____
_____
_____
_____
_____
_____
_____

**CHAPTER NINE**

# LET'S TALK ABOUT BEHAVIOR

Let's face it—anyone who has kids or works with them knows they will have to address behavior at some point. How and why do children learn that negative behavior attracts more attention than positive behavior? We'll probably need to look in the mirror at our reflection to find an answer to this question. Attention is almost always given as a reward for negative behavior by parents and teachers. Not cleaning their room, being rude, making a mess at the table, or leaving their shoes in the middle of the floor will garner words of negative attention from most parents. Talking during class, being late, interfering with another student, not completing assignments, and a variety of other common behaviors are almost certain to gain attention from a teacher. The lesson on how to get adult attention begins as early as infancy. When our children cry, we naturally rush to comfort them. However, when babies play quietly and happily in their playpen or crib, we tend to stay away and enjoy those rare moments of quiet to rest or tend to other matters. They learn as they get older that they will get immediate attention if they throw a toy or hit a sibling. However, if they play quietly with a game or tablet, they are usually left to themselves for a while. These early childhood experiences reinforce the conclusion that negative attention is easier to obtain, even if positive attention is more desired.

*\*Quick note about tablets and other screens: they are not best for young children, even if they are entertaining. As parents, whatever amount of time you decide your child can interact with the screen, try to make it a shared time when possible.*

*Interact with the screen or game together as you would a book and talk about what's happening or sing along to the songs.*

As young people learn to navigate life, parents and teachers want the best for them. But wanting the best does not always mean children will act the best. Children will make mistakes, fall short, and fumble along the way. The growth of challenging behavior in children reflects the rapid changes occurring in the world around us. In a society where almost no one models unconditional compliance with authority, it is difficult to expect students to assume a subservient attitude. Other students have learned not to put their trust in adults. Gone are the days when children could trust any and every adult to be a safe place. Our world has become so dangerous that most parents would caution their children about following the directions of someone just because they are over 21. In addition, the quest for personal power is pervasive.

There will be times when children demonstrate disrespectful behavior that requires attention. While very subjective and open to interpretation, disrespect is a word that most adults identify as a non-negotiable with children. In my opinion, disrespect is any behavior my parents would not have tolerated when I was a child. Behaviors such as eye-rolling, talking back, or ignoring an adult's request to do something. These are behaviors that I, as a parent, do not accept from my children.

Although we try to use encouraging and positive words in most situations, there is language to address negative behaviors. Our response is not to harm a child's self-esteem but will teach, correct, and encourage them in their learning process. When tensions are high, we first must use caution and allow the right words to lower the temperature. If I had followed my advice years ago, I would not have as many regrets as I do about speaking to children when upset. In hindsight, my words had less to do with the child and more with my fear of losing control. My yelling or scolding often demonstrated my lack of control and inability to manage my emotions. Even during moments of correction, an adult's words should teach children and not humiliate or shame them. Positive language can be used when teaching children what we want them to do and what we don't want them to do. Our language can also create boundaries for the child and teach responsibility and accountability. That would be the best lesson for children when we demonstrate how to express our feelings while calmly teaching and addressing behavior.

Let's start with what not to do...

Don't S.T.A.B. the Children!
Scream, Threaten, Argue, or Belittle

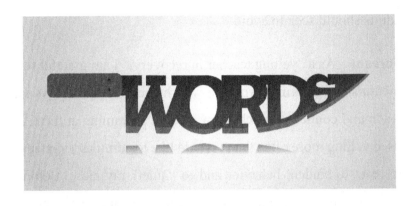

As adults, we would never physically stab children. But the truth is, we can cause just as much harm with our words. Looking back on my early years as a teacher and a mother, I never intended to say anything hurtful or to cause my children or others any shame or embarrassment. Still, occasionally I would STAB them with my words. There were times when I fought to have the last word with a child or screamed at my class that they were my worst class ever. I am not proud of those moments. I am grateful for growth and redemption. In retrospect, my words and actions demonstrated my dissatisfaction, displeasure, or frustration with a child's behavior, which is common when teaching or raising children.

However, remember children will make mistakes, and our job is to help them learn better. This lesson can start with our response to them when they have behaved in an unacceptable way. I use the acronym S.T.A.B. to identify behaviors we as adults should seek to avoid.

**Scream** – As a "yelling teacher in recovery," I am grateful for mentors and a former principal who helped me learn ways to teach and connect with children without screaming at them. I used yelling more often than I would like to admit as a strategy to react to student behavior and to "quiet" my class. Before humans can understand words and their meanings, we respond to tone. If you've ever been yelled at, you know that a loud voice does not make the message clearer. It just demonstrates and sparks heightened emotions. In schools, a raised voice may be necessary when the adult needs to get a large group of students' attention quickly or needs to intervene in a potentially dangerous situation. However, in my experience, screaming and yelling usually occur during a period of heightened emotions, and heightened emotions tend to cloud our judgment. Some sports coaches view yelling as a good coaching technique. Often, their coaches yelled at them when they were young athletes. However, one study on coaching practices suggests that frequent yelling hindered the developmental needs of youth athletes, including a positive sense of self and positive relationships with others (Battaglia et al., 2017)

**Threats** – "If you don't want to do the work, you can leave now, and I will fail you!" These were my words to my fifth-period class. They came into my room, making loud noises, socializing, and ignoring my directions. I was a first-year teacher, and my tolerance level plummeted on this day while my volume skyrocketed. I was so fed up with this "active" ninth-grade class that I seriously considered changing careers. I'd tried everything: quiet signs, pausing instruction, switching seats, but they still treated my class like it was recess. I lost my cool and yelled these words across the classroom. I thought that threatening to fail them would be enough to make them reconsider their disruptive behavior and get back on track. I was wrong. The threat was met with hostility and amusement, and I soon had a class of two since most of the students walked out the door.

Threats create conflict and opposition when the goal is unity and cooperation. Understandably, a tired stressed, and exasperated parent or teacher will resort to threats out of sheer frustration. Commit to not making empty threats. An empty threat is something we never intend to, or would be unethical to, carry out. Failing children is not what I wanted to do, nor could I do it. But even beyond empty threats, threats are not helpful, especially when addressing children in front of their peers. Children, especially adolescents, will often risk everything to "save face" in front of their friends.

**Argue** – Children have a strong desire for power. Arguments are often power struggles. We do whatever we want—at least, that's what children believe. A desire for power is not a bad thing. Growing power needs are a healthy part of child development. Children, particularly as they move toward adolescence, need some freedom to feel and control themselves and their lives to make decisions based on what they believe is best for them. This desire may lead to a child arguing about home rules or classroom expectations. Adults must disengage from the power struggle without winning or giving in. If a child acts childishly, out-childing them isn't the answer. Be the adult. You don't have to fight for your title if you are the teacher or the parent.

Avoid digging into your bag of four-letter words if they throw obscenities at you. When you argue with children, they will believe they are your peer. Show the child how to handle a disagreement or confrontation in a dignified manner while maintaining their dignity and respect. As soon as you notice a power struggle or argument, start de-escalating it and set boundaries. The goal is to focus on solutions rather than continue a debate. Use the following strategies to avoid arguments and maintain a rational approach to communicating with children during conflict:

1. Remember, It Takes Two to Tango – Silence in response to an outburst is often the most respectful thing to do. It's not ignoring what is happening; it's refusing to respond.

1. Use Graceful Exits- Graceful exits describe phrases that aid in de-escalating a power struggle. Graceful exits are closing statements that are said calmly and respectfully during moments of conflict. Graceful exits such as "I hear you," "I will not continue this conversation," "I'm sorry you feel that way," "Good point," or "Let's talk about it later" can help diffuse at the moment while also communicating that the confrontation has ended. For educators, the best way to respond when "on display" in front of other students is to use a simple sentence or two that postpones the resolution of the issue until we are better able to address it. Responses that demonstrate your

professionalism could be another graceful exit. "We can discuss your dislike of my class later," or "Schedule a meeting with me. I look forward to reading your suggestions."

2. Use CARE- The Crisis Prevention Institute suggests using four CARE principles. The four care principles encourage adults to avoid arguing by remembering to:

- **C**oncentrate on the relevant issue.

- **A**cknowledge your active listening through body language.

- **R**espond by paraphrasing and asking questions.

- **E**mphasize your attempt to see things from the other person's perspective.

3. Avoid Accusatory Statements – Phrases such as "You are always late," "I always have to tell you what to do," or "You never stop talking" can spark an argument. These broad accusations are usually very subjective, making the hearer defensive. Consider using more objective and less accusatory statements, such as, "It appears that you are having difficulty getting to my class on time; how can we

fix this?" "What do you think you should do this time?" or "It appears you have a question; how can I assist you?"

**Belittle** – Belittling is the act of making someone else feel worthless, empty, or dismissed.

"You look ridiculous doing that."

or

"You don't know what you are talking about."

When adults react with belittling language, it can shame or embarrass and make a child feel foolish, self-conscious, flustered, or humiliated. Although some adults call this type of language "tough love," belittling can be a covert form of manipulation or emotional abuse. "Constantly belittling, threatening or ignoring children can be as damaging to their mental health as physical or sexual abuse" (Goodwin, 2012). When someone belittles another, they frequently trivialize, minimize, downgrade, or play down another's personhood or feelings. This leads to feeling unimportant, inferior, or minimized.

We must seek to model self-control with our language choices and set an example for our children. Modeling this level of control will help them as they enter adulthood and learn to interact with a supervisor, a future spouse, or an aggressive driver.

Here are language choices that can be beneficial:

**Restorative Language** – restorative language relies on dialogue to repair relationships. It involves discussions about discipline. Restorative language in schools and classrooms requires intentional and respectful speaking and listening by everyone involved. According to the International Institute of Restorative Practices (IIRP), restorative questions are used to process an incident of wrongdoing or conflict.

Examples of Restorative Questions

1. "What happened?"

2. "What were you thinking at the time of the incident?"

3. "What have you thought about since?"

4. "Who has been affected by what happened and how?"

5. "What about this has been the hardest for you?"

6. "What do you think needs to be done to make things right?

Restorative questions lead to conversations between people following an incident that caused concern to one or more people. With restorative language, adults treat challenging situations differently from traditional models that promote immediate punishment. Restorative language promotes speaking and listening by encouraging open dialogue. Listeners take a neutral stance and seek to assist the individual in making decisions. Parties accept responsibility for their actions and determine what needs to be done to make things right. Restorative conversations focus on solutions rather than punishing and blaming.

**Affective Statements** – affective statements are also used in restorative conversations to communicate a need, feeling, or observation. Sometimes called "I" statements, they emphasize our feelings or beliefs rather than assign blame to the other person. Children better understand others' emotions and feelings when parents and teachers use affective statements. Affective statements are often taught in social-emotional learning and restorative practice programs to help children share their feelings with another student who demonstrated less than positive behavior. However, affective statements are also beneficial for adults when dealing with conflict. I have witnessed many examples of students being approached with an accusatory tone of blame and threatened with punishment. The student often responds with a wave of negative emotions and defensiveness that can trigger an escalation of problem behavior. Affective statements are tools teachers can use when a minor conflict arises with a student. Affective statements provide a way for the adult to share frustration with the behavior the student has demonstrated. They follow a format such as:

I noticed I felt... (the emotion) when... (the occurrence). It makes it (reason) because _____.

Affective statements can also include a statement of need and a plan or request.

> *"I feel upset when you neglect to empty the dishwasher because we cannot keep the sink clean. Please do it now."*

> *"I feel annoyed when you call out in class because it distracts your classmates. Please raise your hand."*

Affective statements can also highlight a virtue or character trait that they exhibited.

> *"Thank you for demonstrating responsibility by emptying the dishwasher."*
>
> *"Thank you for showing self-control by raising your hand."*

Affective statements are not limited to correcting behavior but can also be used to teach and reinforce positive actions and behavior. Examples are as follows:

> *"I noticed that you apologized to Jalen. I am delighted that you chose to do this when you bumped into him. That shows that you understand that your behavior could have hurt him."*
>
> *"I noticed that you held the door open for Marta. I was thankful that you chose to help. It shows you are being respectful."*
>
> *"I am excited to see you working through that complex math problem. You were able to use strategies that were previously taught."*

Because you're now talking with the student rather than at them, this simple change can help you build a relationship. The affective statements are not judgmental, which aids in maintaining positive relationships even in the face of conflict.

## When/Then Language

The when/then language is used when we give a child a less preferred activity or a low-probability behavior. Then, offer them a highly preferred activity or a high-probability behavior. The child is likelier to do the less preferred activity if it is attached to "when and then." Put "when" you do this (a task you don't like or that is hard), "then" you get that (a motivating or preferred activity or reward). When we want children to remember the importance of doing what is required before a more desirable activity, a "when-then" phrase is ideal. For example, "When you brush your teeth, we can play the game," or "When you finish your homework, you can have your phone." Brushing teeth and doing homework might be the less preferred activities, but by using the when/then, the child is learning the lesson we want to instill. Do what you **have to** do before you do what you **want to** do.

Teachers can also use the phrase to help children know what is expected. The focus is less on the undesirable behavior but on what the desired activity might be.

> "When you are quiet, then we will leave for lunch."

> "When you turn in your first draft, then you will get more feedback on your request for an extension on your final paper."

In this example, being quiet and completing the first draft are the required activity, and the desired activity is going to lunch and an extension.

I have seen other versions of this type of language referred to as "grandma's law." This version uses " if " instead of "when." The statement would be, "If you are quiet, we will leave for lunch." This method is based on the image of a grandmother who encourages her grandchildren to finish their vegetables in a sweet soft voice, "Darling, if you finish your spinach, then you can have a cookie." I don't know about anyone else, but that was not my grandmother's style. She was not into bribery. When we regularly announce rewards as a gift of compliance, it can border on bribery. She would clearly and directly tell me, "When you finish your dinner, then you can get up from the table." I prefer "when" for two reasons. First, it gives the directive in a straightforward yet respectful way. Second, it does not open the conversation window for children to discuss "if" they are going to do something. We can remain calm, provide directions, and project the expectation that our requests will be fulfilled.

Please and Thank you

At its most basic, using the words please and thank you shows respect and consideration. Good Manners are a social norm and a powerful way to build relationships, model good character, and communicate a genuine appreciation.

## Takeaways

- Use language that does not seek to damage a child's self-esteem but will continue to teach and encourage them.

- Accountability and grace can coexist when children make mistakes.

- Restorative language and affective statements promote dialogue, reinforce positive actions, and explain feelings without assigning blame or shame.

- The adage goes, "You have to give respect to get respect." When we are polite and say *please*, children are likelier to model the same language and demonstrate respect.

## Pause for Reflection

What behaviors would you categorize as disrespectful from your child or your students? Are these behaviors consistent with what you were taught as a child?

_____

_____

_____

_____

Create an affective statement to address behavior that you have seen recently with your child or your student.

_____

_____

_____

_____

_____

_____

Respond—Don't React with Words

In my early years of teaching, I felt like I was playing a game of Whack-A-Mole when dealing with student behaviors. I would wait for a student to do something wrong and react to the behavior with whatever words or actions my mind produced. My reaction was often based on whatever emotion I felt about the behavior: mad, frustrated, irritated, or even exasperated. For example, one day, a student in one of my classrooms yelled, "I don't want to be in this class! It's boring!" My response was just as sharp. "Well, I don't want you here, either. Get out!" I'd taken the student's outburst personally, like a slap in the face, and my reaction was to respond in kind. The student went to the office, and I got to have a conference with his mother. Not the outcome that either of us wanted.

It doesn't mean we don't feel emotions when we respond instead of reacting; it just means that what we choose is based on our feelings is different. When we are "triggered" by a child or anyone's behavior, we realize that our immediate reaction may make us feel good for a moment, let off some steam, or attempt to assert our assumed authority. Still, it may not help us to achieve our goal. I have asked parents to name times they were triggered and reacted instead of responding to their child. "When my child was moving too slow to get ready for school," "When I had to say the same thing repeatedly," or "When they chose to argue with me over a rule." Interestingly, similar answers came from educators who described the last time they felt they reacted instead of responded to student behavior. Examples such as "When I ask them to do something, and they completely ignore me," "When I've had to repeat directions many times," or "When they give me attitude about following school rules."

"Sasha, I'd appreciate it if you could put away your phone and place it in your bag," a teacher asked the eighth grader when she entered the classroom. The teacher walked away, leaving

Sasha to make the right decision. Sasha completely ignored the request and continued to use her phone. The teacher lost her temper, and Sasha appeared confused. In this situation, emotions can get the best of us if we let them. "How dare you act as if you didn't hear me!" was probably her gut reaction. Her fight, flight, or freeze button was activated. Ignoring is a hot button for me as well. But I had to learn to control it and not let students cause me to lose control.

Parents may deal with the same behavior from children or adolescents at home. My emotional reaction as a parent would be the same, but my response would be different. I would immediately take the phone and inform her that her memories of her phone would be the only thing she would carry for a long time. However, when it comes to students' personal space and property, educators must tread a different path.

According to Dr. Marc Brackett, author of *Permission to Feel (2019)*, "triggered" is a telling word to describe how we react to our emotions. We say it as though there's something outside of us pulling a trigger—your child talks back in a rude tone or stomps her foot, which triggers your anger. But the trigger is inside us, not out there, and we can choose to disable our trigger points. The difference between responding and reacting is that reactions can negatively impact you or others, whereas responding can provide the opportunity to teach and move forward. In a nutshell, responding is emotional intelligence, while reacting is just emotional.

QTIP—Quit Taking It Personally. When we take the behavior personally, we are more likely to react and not respond positively. But how do we respond to the behavior and not react to the child? First, we must be proactive. I coached the teacher to address the cell phone policy at the beginning of class when she greeted all the students. "Welcome; please be sure to put your cell phones away and take out your Chromebook. I appreciate your cooperation." A personal request will follow if the student fails to follow the stated direction. If the behavior continues, choose whether you will discuss the situation later or present a consequence, but either choice is a response, not a reaction. Occasionally, our children observe when we tell them to be responsible and calm and then ignore our advice when faced with conflict.

Critique vs. Criticism

In my first book, *School Smart* (2017), I refer to teachers and parents as coaches for children as they learn and play the game of life. While coaching our players, we innately do what many coaches and sideline fans are well-versed in: we offer criticism. Adults play a significant role in teaching children how to accept feedback healthily by balancing critiques and negative criticism.

According to a study on parental expression, children who have critical parents learn to pay less attention to faces that express any emotion (James et al., 2018). This limits their ability to "read" people effectively, which is necessary for establishing and maintaining relationships. According to the authors, children who receive a lot of criticism tend to avoid positive and negative facial expressions as an adaptive measure to avoid the feelings that come with it. This makes sense because we are hardwired to gravitate toward what feels safe and away from what may cause us harm. Anything that calls our inherent "goodness" into question counts as harm. Furthermore, these children also begin to expect criticism not only from their parents, but also from others. This demonstrates that our words impact how a child interprets the intentions, needs, and desires of others, as well as their feelings toward us.

This does not imply that we should always try to avoid unpleasant words or responses to children's behavior. Children must be addressed and corrected numerous times and must learn to accept feedback, direction, and critique from adults. However, we should learn ways to correct and give feedback to children in a manner that includes compassion and patience, allowing them to explore the lessons they need to learn without shattering their sense of self. Instead of focusing solely on their flaws, it means communicating with them in a way they can understand. Instead of only offering harsh criticism that seeks to judge and place blame, use words to critique a child's behavior and offer room for growth and improvement.

## Takeaways

- Children who receive a lot of criticism tend to avoid positive and negative facial expressions as an adaptive measure to avoid the feelings that come with it.

- When responding to defiant behavior or power struggles, make brief yet direct statements. Avoid lectures and sarcasm.

- Children want their own power, not yours. Use words to offer guidance, choices, and boundaries.

- Commit not to use words that are harmful or demeaning to not just children but to humans.

## Reflection

When is it most difficult for you to model positive language with children? (Time of day, feeling/emotion?)

_____

_____

_____

_____

_____

_____

_____

_____

_____

## CHAPTER TEN

# INTENT VS. IMPACT OF WORDS

The intent of our words refers to the message we mean to convey. The impact of the words refers to how the other person perceives them. We want to model for children that regardless of the intention of our words, it is the impact that matters. If something we do or say negatively impacts another person or group of people, our intention is less critical. We must recognize our impact and correct our words or actions moving forward. As parents and educators, we must recognize that our choice of words may send the wrong message even if our intentions are good. Whether correct or incorrect, a child's perception shapes beliefs that influence their learning, behavior, and identity. Below are examples of language often used with one intent while leading to a different impact on children.

## Sarcasm

I am not bilingual, but I am fluent in sarcasm. Sarcastic responses such as, "Nice job," "Very funny," or "That was smart" can easily flow from my mouth. Maybe I learned it from the television shows I watched over the years. My all-time favorite show is *The Golden Girls*. This 80's TV sitcom features Bea Arthur, Estelle Getty, Betty White, and Rue McClanahan. The show, which won several awards, continues to be a fan favorite years into syndication. Much of the show's success was due to the four senior ladies' hilarious comebacks and sarcastic responses. Used respectfully, I believe sarcasm can provide humor and even improve communication in healthy relationships.

**SARCASTIC COMMENT**

Loading...
PLEASE WAIT

*Intent vs. Impact of Words*

Yet, proceed with great caution in this area with children. In the spirit of the saying, "It's not what you say, it's how you say it," adults who use sarcasm with young children risk being misunderstood at best and creating long-term scars at worst. Sarcasm is often hard to understand for young children. When an adult uses sarcasm, they say something different from, and often opposite to, what they really mean. When my son was in the second grade, he was talking in class at a time when he should not have been. His teacher sarcastically said, "Matthew, the class will wait until you have finished talking," thinking Matthew would understand his sarcasm and cease his conversation. My son responded, "Okay, thank you," and continued talking to his friend. Now, you must know my son Matthew to know that he is not a rule breaker nor a child who would willfully disrespect his teacher. At seven years old, he took his teacher's words literally and thought she would allow him to continue talking.

The Greek root of sarcasm originally meant to "tear flesh." Ouch!!! The current English word (sarcasm. 2011. In *Merriam-Webster*, 2011) is a "satirical or ironic utterance designed to cut or give pain." We may think our words are harmless when taken at face value, but some may come off as passive-aggressive comments. When sarcasm is used to manipulate, it can cause unintentional hurt, embarrassment, or pain. When I was sarcastic, I never meant to hurt anyone. However, the impact of our words is more important than our intent. Some children are sensitive and respond negatively to sarcasm, even if we have the best intentions. Tread lightly.

## Comforting Words

1. "Bless your heart."
2. "A lot of people struggle with this concept."
3. "You have other skills."
4. "Not everyone is cut out to do geometry."
5. "Don't worry. I knew this would be hard for some of you."

Evidence demonstrates that "comforting words" are a strong demotivator of excellence (Rattan et al., 2012). Bias and limiting mindsets may be demonstrated using "comforting words." These well-meaning phrases and "comforting words" can have serious consequences for children struggling academically or socially. An adult who tells a child to focus on their strengths and accept their weaknesses is not as encouraging as you might think. It may demonstrate a limiting belief about a child's potential. Regular use of "comforting words" with children who are struggling can result in situations that influence children to abandon new skills or advanced fields of study. Their brain changes their "goal representation" and then focuses on a different, more modest goal. Americans underperform students in other countries in math and science and are less likely to pursue advanced degrees in math- and science-related fields (National Science Foundation, 2010). Educators and parents have a critical role in encouraging male and female students from all backgrounds to persist and maintain their academic engagement. A student's prediction of their success strongly predicts how well they perform. Our words should help children to raise the bar rather than lower it.

## "Why" and Other Rhetorical Questions

"Sir, why are you speeding?" This accusatory "why" question comes from a highway patrol officer that pulls over a speeding driver. The question appears to be looking for information. However, the actual message is unmistakable. It means "GOTCHA!! I've caught you doing something wrong, and I'm going to let you dig a bigger hole for yourself by allowing you to lie while I run your tags or prepare to write you a ticket." Any response to the question "why" you were speeding is an admission that you were speeding. This can be used in court against you if you attempt to contest the speeding ticket.

Have you ever asked a child, "Why did you do that?" "Why are you talking?" "Why is your room a mess?" or "Why are you running in the hall?" If so, consider if you are looking for the reason for the behavior or if you want to let the child know you caught them doing wrong. Is your why question usually the start of your lectures and reminders?

A rhetorical question is a question that is merely for effect, with no answer expected. They can often begin as a why question but can also take on other forms. A parent stressing the importance of achieving in school might question their high school senior, "Do you want to live here in the basement for the rest of your life?" hoping the child will realize that good grades lead to a good-paying job. The problem with rhetorical questions is that they often create barriers. The teen will stare blankly or offer the ever-so-popular response, "I don't know." Rhetorical questions are frequently like passive-aggressive conversations. We often make the person feel silly about their actions, even if that is not our intention. Unfortunately, rhetorical questions can also block meaningful communication, and neither party feels they've gotten their point across. Questions such as, "What's your problem?" or "Did you think before you did that?" are often asked to make children feel bad about their decision-making processes.

Worse, some rhetorical questions breed facetious or flippant responses. For instance, a question such as "How many times do I have to tell you...?" could elicit the response, "Twenty times." The conversation becomes a tug-of-war, a disciplinary response, or a spark for an argument.

## Takeaways

- Learning to understand sarcasm is difficult for most children.

- "Comforting words" can be a strong demotivator of excellence.

- The impact of our words is more important than the intent of our words.

- Avoid rhetorical questions. Say what you mean and mean what you say.

## Moment of Reflection

Have you ever used "comforting words" like those presented with a child? If so, was it to console or stretch them to do more?

_____
_____
_____
_____
_____
_____
_____

Do you use sarcasm when communicating with children? In what context?

_____
_____
_____
_____
_____
_____
_____
_____

**CHAPTER ELEVEN**

# SPEAKING HOPE TO OUR CHILDREN

I'm sure you'd agree that we want the next generation to succeed and go further than we have. We must equip and motivate our children to do their best for this to happen. We want our children to have hope. Hope is not merely a wishy-washy, touchy-feely emotion. When the word "hope" is misused to describe something like "I hope I win the lottery"

or "I hope it doesn't rain," it implies a lack of agency or control over the outcome. This is not what I mean when speaking about language that gives children hope. Everyone has access to hope, which is a fundamental human strength. Hope is composed of cognitive and affective factors, and our language can assist children in developing both.

> *"Hope is the belief that your future can be brighter and better than your past and that you have a role to play in making it better."*
> **~ Casey Gwinn**

Research shows that the common factor in determining a child's future success is if they have stable, committed, healthy relationships with adults in their lives (Cohen, 2017). The relationships can be with parents, teachers, coaches, mentors, or other trusted adults. Through national programs such as Kids Hope USA and 100 Black Men of America, mentors are provided to K-12 students, and hope is fostered. Through Kids Hope USA, Aiden met his mentor Ms. Stacie. They met every Wednesday, and that day quickly became Aiden's favorite day of the week. From first grade through middle school, Aidan met with Ms. Stacie for one hour each week. She became a trusted friend, his second mom, and one of his biggest cheerleaders. According to Aiden and his mom, many life lessons emerged from their relationship, and they became hopeful messages that lived on with Aiden. They included:

1. Always work hard and do your best.
2. Don't forget to make time for fun.
3. Find joy in simple things.
4. Smile... it's contagious.
5. Never give up!

Bryce met with his mentor one Saturday each month for six years through the mentorship program with 100 Black Men of America. Bryce, a high school senior, comments, "Looking back, it was one of the best decisions my mother could have made for me. I was exposed to guest speakers, career professionals, dignitaries, and politicians." Bryce credits his mentorship with helping him to move forward in his future. All children should feel hopeful about their future no matter their circumstances. Even in the face of adversity and uncertainty, hope can survive and thrive. Communicating and fostering hope in social settings, including hospitals and non-profits (like the Ronald McDonald House), have been helpful for parents with children with serious health problems. Research has shown that hopeful language can help parents find care solutions, encourage, and set goals for their children's lives, and maintain their children's quality of life. (Rafferty, et al, 2020).

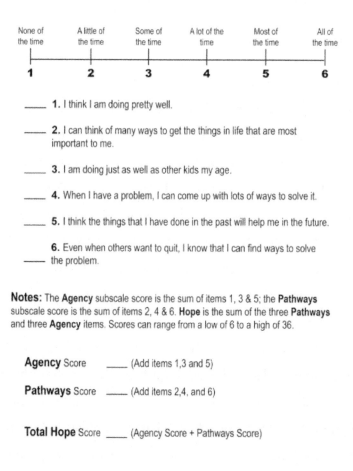

## Speaking Hope to Our Children

So, how can we tell if our kids are high on hope? C.R. Snyder, a psychologist who theorized that much of human behavior was goal-directed, created the Children's Hope Scale. (Gwinn & Hellman, 2018) Children who can identify paths toward their goals and have the willpower to sustain goal-directed motivation are considered hopeful. He created a six-item self-report survey of pathways and agency thinking specifically for children ages 8-16 (See Hope Scale).

Use language to help children consider the kind of world they want to live in. What kind of family do they want to have? Where do they want to live? Hope can point them in the direction of their desired future. When we say, "When you graduate" vs. "If you graduate," or "When you earn your degree" vs. "If you earn a degree," we show them that we believe in them. Our encouraging messages will stay with them when we show them how their decisions affect them today and tomorrow.

The aspirational question "What do you want to be when you grow up?" is a fixed way of thinking about the future. It implies that they will select a single career, train for it, and devote their lives to it. It would be far better to encourage students to adopt a growth mindset, encourage their curiosity, and emphasize that continuous learning will be a requirement of adulthood.

Instead of asking children, "What do you want to be when you grow up?" allow them to explore different career options and discover the path necessary for each.

According to academic coach Chris Logan, there are better questions than "What Do you want to do when you grow up?" that adults can ask to foster hope and support lifelong learning for children. They include:

> *"What are some things you'd like to do, experience, or accomplish in your life?"*

> *"What jobs do you think are common now that won't exist in the future? What jobs that don't exist now might come into being?"*

> *"What kinds of things do you enjoy learning? What are you curious about?"*

> *"What types of projects and puzzles interest you?"*

> *"Is there anything you'd like to try or experience before you go to college? How can I support that?"*

> *"What are some of the problems facing our world that you might like to help solve? How can you get involved right now?"*

Regardless of the current state of our world, I pray that my children can find reasons to be hopeful. Author Dr. Eric Jensen reminds educators, "How much hope and optimism your kids feel at your school is more important for boosting achievement than their IQ; without it, all other strategies will fail" (2022). As adults, we influence a child's sense of hope. This is not a "false hope" that ignores the laundry list of traumas, inequities, and stressors that many children face. Schools will be unable to successfully transition students into a better future if we ignore the environments in which some of our students live and the factors that influence their lives outside of the classroom. Toxic stress, poverty, violence, racism, and sexism are all prevalent and impact children's development of hope. We have children today who are not just anxious but downright discouraged. Who could blame them? As much as we try to shield children from the challenges in the wider world, they are aware of deadly pandemics, wars, injustices, natural disasters, and other stressors.

While it is true that "children are resilient," their resilience is dependent on the support and teaching of those around them who can help them learn to navigate both good and challenging times. We don't just want our children to bounce back from adversity. We want them to move forward with new goals and the ability to overcome obstacles and barriers that may still exist. Teaching hope entails more than just being compassionate and supportive. We can teach children fundamental skills that will enable them to take control of their lives. We can teach children how to set realistic goals, have a positive outlook, navigate adversity, and contribute positively to society. Kids need us to gain the self-assurance needed to maintain an "I can do it" attitude. Words of hope focus on the future, where the possibilities are plenty. We use them to remind children that things do not have to stay as they are. Words like "Tomorrow will be better" and "You have the power to make a choice" let children know that what they do deserves focus, not the circumstances outside their control. Every child should have hope. That is what I want for my children, the children in my community, and the children in your community. All children need and deserve hope.

## Takeaways

- Hope is a fundamental human strength that everyone has access to.

- Hope is one of the most significant predictors of student success.

- Adults can use language to foster hope in children by supporting their agency and motivation levels for their present and future goals.

## Reflection

Review the Hope Scale and consider the hope that you may have had as a child and how the relationships with trusted adults may have impacted your hope level.

_____
_____
_____
_____
_____
_____
_____
_____
_____

*Children Are Listening*

# CLOSING WORDS

*"It is not our job to toughen our children up to face a cruel and heartless world. It's our job to raise children who will make the world a little less cruel and heartless."*
**~ L. R. Knost**

"Sticks and stones may break my bones, but words can never hurt me." This saying should be listed as one of the biggest untruths next to "if you cross your eyes, they will get stuck that way." Words can scar and leave pain long after a stick or stone bruises. We would never break children's bones with sticks and stones, yet our words are just as powerful. Words can be tools of torture or vehicles of encouragement and hope. Whether you are a parent talking to your children or an educator talking to your students, what we say to them can make all the difference in the world. Our choice of words can help an uncertain child feel more confident. They can help a child who feels lonely and isolated reach out to others. Words spoken mindfully help children take the initiative needed to tackle academic challenges.

I hope this book will help us find confidence and success… our own and that of our young people. The goal is not to make you feel that you have been using the "wrong" words with children or using poor communication skills. Great parents and teachers have been known to ask rhetorical questions, raise their voices, and use sarcasm. I know I have. These moments are valuable learning moments too.

Using language that builds confidence, optimism, and resilience in our children can become second nature with deliberate effort. Neuroplasticity refers to our brain's ability to change and adapt because of our experiences or new learning. When learning, significant changes occur in your brain, including creating new connections between your neurons (Blanchette Sarrasin et al., 2020). Previously, science supported the premise that the brain stopped changing after age 25, at which point the brain was fully wired and mature. At that point, they thought it was all downhill. Fortunately, this grim view of the aging brain has been put to rest. We now know that the human brain is capable of change throughout life. The adult brain can create new neuronal connections and even new

## Closing Words

neurons, but it doesn't happen without work. We, like our children, can grow and change! The great news is that our brains can and do change throughout our lives, and we all have room to grow and change. If you have made a misstep, don't beat yourself up. Set a goal to learn better and do better.

I hope this book has sparked positive thoughts and actions in you, leading to intentionality in our interactions with children. "It takes a village to raise a child" is an African proverb that means that an entire community of people must provide for and interact positively with children for those children to experience and grow in a safe and healthy environment. Let's continue to build the children in our villages with intentional words of hope that can lead them to become positive and productive members of our society. Children are listening, and what we say matters.

*Children Are Listening*

# 37 PHRASES CHILDREN NEED TO HEAR FROM ADULTS

(Partial list compiled from participants from my What We Say Matters workshop)

1. You've got what it takes.

2. This is your responsibility.

3. I'm proud of you.

4. I believe in you.

5. I understand how you feel.

6. You are not your mistakes.

7. You can do this.

8. This family, class, or school is better because you are here

9. I'm glad that you are here.

10. I'm sorry.

11. I'm listening.

12. It's good to see you today.

13. You are safe with me.

14. I forgive you.

15. The answer is no.

16. I see you.

17. You're important to me.

18. That's a great idea!

19. I'm proud of the way you handled that.

20. Try that again.

21. Mistakes happen.

22. I love you.

23. I know this is hard, but you can do hard things.

24. Go Play

25. Not everyone will like you.

26. What do you think?

27. What did you learn today?

28. Teach me how you did that.

29. I'm here for you

30. Let me see your homework

31. What will you do differently next time?

32. You can tell me anything.

33. When I'm struggling, I like to…

34. I appreciate you.

35. Don't Give Up

36. Make Good Choices.

37. God Loves You

## BEFORE YOU GO

If you laughed, learned, or enjoyed this book in any way, I'm so glad! I hope you're glad you picked it up or found it useful in some way. I appreciate your time, your insights, and your tips. Thank you. If you have found this book worth reading for any reason, I would really appreciate your leaving an honest review on Amazon, or dropping me an email about your own tips, ideas, and stories. I have more books on the horizon and would love to include the wisdom of my peers!

Please share, give, or lend your copy to a colleague, parent, or anyone who connects with children. They should know the power of their words can change the life of a child.

With Gratitude,

*Shauna*

shauna@shaunafking.com
www.shaunafking.com
www.classroomsofhope.com

# REFERENCES

Amen, D. G., & Amen, T. (2017). *The brain warrior's way: Ignite your energy and focus, attack illness and aging, transform pain into purpose.* Penguin Publishing Group.

Battaglia, A. V., Kerr, G., & Stirling, A. E. (2017). Youth athletes' interpretations of punitive coaching practices. *Journal of Applied Sport Psychology, 29*(3), 337–352. https://doi.org/10.1080/10413200.2016.1271370

Biondi, C.-A. (2018, August 30). *Marva Collins, her method, and her 'philosophy for living'.* The Objective Standard. https://theobjectivestandard.com/2018/08/marva-collins-her-method-and-her-philosophy-for-living/

Blanchette Sarrasin, J., Brault Foisy, L.-M., Allaire-Duquette, G., & Masson, S. (2020). Understanding your brain to help you learn better. *Frontiers for Young Minds, 8*, 54. https://doi.org/10.3389/frym.2020.00054

Brackett, M. (2019). *Permission to feel: Unlocking the power of emotions to help our kids, ourselves, and our society thrive.* Celadon Books.

Bowen, W. (2009). *Complaint free relationships: How to positively transform your personal, work, and love relationships.* Harmony.

Cobb, F., & Krownapple, J. (2019). *Belonging through a culture of dignity: the keys to successful equity implementation.* Mimi & Todd Press.

Cohen, S. D. (2017). *Three principles to improve outcomes for children and families. Science to policy and practice* (Science to Policy and Practice). Center on the Developing Child at Harvard University. https://eric.ed.gov/?id=ED583256

Conor, S. (2016, November 20). Is pessimism really bad for you? *The Guardian.* https://www.theguardian.com/society/2016/nov/20/is-pessimism-bad-for-you

Cook, C. R., Grady, E. A., Long, A. C., Renshaw, T., Codding, R. S., Fiat, A., & Larson, M. (2017). Evaluating the impact of increasing general education teachers' ratio of positive-to-negative interactions on students' classroom behavior. *Journal of Positive Behavior Interventions, 19*(2), 67–77. https://doi.org/10.1177/1098300716679137

# References

Dweck, C. S. (2008). *Mindset: The new psychology of success* (Updated ed.). Ballantine Books.

Esparza, J., Shumow, L., & Schmidt, J. A. (2014). Growth mindset of gifted seventh grade students in science. *NCSSSMST Journal, 19*(1), 6–13. http://files.eric.ed.gov/fulltext/EJ1045824.pdf

Feldman, D. (2014). *The heart of education: Bringing joy, meaning and purpose back to teaching and learning.* Motivational Press.

Garcia, O., Kleifgen, J. A., & Falchi, L. (2008). *From English language learners to emergent bilinguals* (Equity Matters: Research Review No. 1). New York. Teachers College, Columbia University. https://files.eric.ed.gov/fulltext/ED524002.pdf

Greenlaw, E. (2021, April 29). Talking to your child about slurs: When words hurt. *Answers: Your Destination for Kids' Health,* Boston Children's Hospital. https://answers.childrenshospital.org/talking-about-slurs/

Guimarães, D. M., Valério-Gomes, B., & Lent, R. (2020). Neuroplasticity: The brain changes over time. *Frontiers for Young Minds, 8,* 521413. https://doi.org/10.3389/frym.2020.522413

Gwinn, C., & Hellman, C. (2018). *Hope rising: How the science of hope can change your life*. Morgan James Publishing.

Hammond, Z. (with Jackson, Y.). (2015). *Culturally responsive teaching and the brain: Promoting authentic engagement and rigor among culturally and linguistically diverse students*. Corwin.

Harris, B. (2020). *17 things resilient teachers do (and 4 things they hardly ever do)*. Routledge.

Hussong, A. M., Langley, H. A., Thomas, T., Coffman, J., Halberstadt, A., Costanzo, P., & Rothenberg, W. A. (2019). Measuring gratitude in children. *The Journal of Positive Psychology, 14*(5), 563–575. https://doi.org/10.1080/17439760.2018.1497692

James, K. M., Owens, M., Woody, M. L., Hall, N. T., & Gibb, B. E. (2018). Parental expressed emotion-criticism and neural markers of sustained attention to emotional faces in children. *Journal of Clinical Child & Adolescent Psychology, 47*(sup1), S520-S529.

Jensen, E. (2022). *Teaching with poverty and equity in mind*. ASCD.

# References

Knost, L. R. (2013). *Two thousand kisses a day: Gentle parenting through the ages and stages.* Little Hearts Books.

Luedtke, H. S. (2019, December 7). *How to encourage optimism and positive thoughts in children.* Metro Parent. https://www.metroparent.com/parenting/advice/encourage-optimism-positive-thoughts-children/

Masten, A. S., & Barnes, A. J. (2018). Resilience in children: Developmental perspectives. *Children, 5*(7), 98. https://doi.org/10.3390/children5070098

Merriam-Webster. (n.d.). Sarcasm. In *Merriam-Webster.com dictionary.* Retrieved October 30, 2022, from https://www.merriam-webster.com/dictionary/sarcasm

Pahlke, E., Bigler, R. S., & Suizzo, M.-A. (2012). Relations between colorblind socialization and children's racial bias: Evidence from European American mothers and their preschool children. *Child Development, 83*(4), 1164–1179. https://doi.org/10.1111/j.1467-8624.2012.01770.x

Rafferty, K.A., Beck, G.A., & McGuire, M. (2020). When Facing Hopeful and Hopeless Experiences: Using Snyder's Hope Theory to Understand Parents' Caregiving Experiences for Their Medically Complex Child. *Journal of pediatric health care: official publication of National Association of Pediatric Nurse Associates & Practitioners*.

Rattan, A., Good, C., & Dweck, C. S. (2012). "It's ok—Not everyone can be good at math": Instructors with an entity theory comfort (and demotivate) students. *Journal of experimental social psychology, 48*(3), 731-737.

Romeo, R. R., Leonard, J. A., Robinson, S. T., West, M. R., Mackey, A. P., Rowe, M. L., & Gabrieli, J. D. E. (2018). Beyond the 30-million-word gap: children's conversational exposure is associated with language-related brain function. *Psychological Science, 29*(5), 700–710. https://doi.org/10.1177/0956797617742725

Rudasill, K. M. (2011). Child temperament, teacher–child interactions, and teacher–child relationships: A longitudinal investigation from first to third grade. *Early Childhood Research Quarterly, 26*(2), 147–156. https://doi.org/10.1016/j.ecresq.2010.07.002

Sackstein, S. (2016, February 14). *Shifting the grading mindset starts with our words.* Education Week. https://www.edweek.org/leadership/opinion-shifting-the-grading-mindset-starts-with-our-words/2016/02

Sadker, M., & Sadker, D. (1985). Sexism in the Classroom. *Vocational Education Journal, 60*(7), 30-32.

Salleh, M. R. (2008). Life event, stress and illness. *The Malaysian Journal of Medical Sciences, 15*(4), 9–18.

Seligman, M. E. P. (2006). *Learned optimism: How to change your mind and your life.* Vintage Books.

Souers, K., & Hall, P. A. (2016). *Fostering resilient learners: Strategies for creating a trauma-sensitive classroom.* ASCD.

Thomas, C. R., & Gadbois, S. A. (2007). Academic self-handicapping: The role of self-concept clarity and students' learning strategies. *The British Journal of Educational Psychology, 77*(1), 101–119. https://doi.org/10.1348/000709905X79644

Willoughby, B. (2018). *Speak up at school: How to respond to everyday prejudice, bias and stereotypes* (Teaching tolerance publication). Montgomery, Alabama. Southern Poverty Law Center.

Made in the USA
Middletown, DE
06 April 2023

27928455R00086